GORGIAS

Plato

GORGIAS

Translated, with
Introduction and Notes, by

DONALD J. ZEYL

HACKETT PUBLISHING COMPANY
Indianapolis/Cambridge

Plato: *ca* 428–347 B.C.

Printed in the United States of America
10 09 08 07 8 9 10 11

Interior design by J. M. Matthew
Cover design by Listenberger Design and Associates

For further information, please address

Hackett Publishing Company, Inc.
P.O. Box 44937
Indianapolis, IN 46244-0937

www.hackettpublishing.com

Library of Congress Cataloging-in-Publication Data

Plato.
Gorgias.
Bibliography: p.
1. Ethics. 2. Political science—Early works to 1700. I. Zeyl, Donald J., 1944– II. Title.
B371.A5Z48 1986 170 86014946
ISBN 0-87220-017-5
ISBN 0-87220-016-7 (pbk.)

ISBN-13: 978-0-87220-017-3 (cloth)
ISBN-13: 978-0-87220-016-6 (pbk.)

Contents

For Judy

Acknowledgments

As the publisher's readers, Daniel Devereux and Richard Kraut made many helpful criticisms and suggestions. I am especially indebted to Kraut's thorough, line-by-line check of the translation against the Greek text and his sensitive and sensible comments. The translation owes much to his careful study. James B. Atkinson, the copy editor, made many valuable suggestions to improve the English style. My best thanks are due to the late William Hackett, who suggested this translation project to me and who gave me every encouragement. I deeply regret that he did not live to see its publication.

Kingston, Rhode Island DONALD J. ZEYL

Introduction

Plato's *Gorgias* begins with an examination of the character and claims of oratory, and ends with a passionate exhortation to choose the life of the philosopher over that of the orator-politician. As we read through the dialogue, we observe Plato raising with ever increasing intensity a host of questions that reveal the connections between oratory and a way of life of which it is an external expression, a way of life that Plato sees as thoroughly reprehensible. As the moral implications of the practice of oratory are developed in the course of Socrates' successive discussions with Gorgias, Polus, and Callicles, all three of whom are champions of oratory and in varying degrees committed to the corresponding way of life, Plato juxtaposes to and contrasts with that life the life of the philosopher.[1]

We will not appreciate Plato's forceful denunciation of oratory if we fail to understand the importance of oratory in

[1]The Greek moral philosophers typically held that the basic alternatives for ethical choice are alternative lives, or ways of life. One's choice among such ways of life is to be rationally determined by considering which of the alternatives has the better claim to being identified as the happy *(eudaimon)* life—the life that is most worthwhile for a human being to live. The conditions that in turn define the most worthwhile human life are generally derived from the philosopher's account of the nature of the human soul (see Plato, *Republic* 4 and 9; Aristotle, *Nicomachean Ethics*, 1 and 10).

the social and political life of fifth-century Athens. In the major institutions of the democracy in Athens, such as the Assembly, the Council, and the law courts, decisions were made by the vote of the membership of those bodies. Anyone who had a right to speak and who possessed the skill of speaking persuasively before such a body thus had the opportunity to influence deliberation and hence the outcome of the vote in the direction of his own interests. Hence oratory was, and was recognized to be, an extremely powerful instrument for attaining one's personal ambitions. It is easy to see why the successful orator became an object of admiration and envy.

It may be helpful to see how the contrast between the way of life of the orator-politician and that of the philosopher is drawn in the dialogue. An external difference between them is their mode of speaking, and Plato makes this difference apparent almost immediately in the dialogue. The orator has a penchant for long, uninterrupted, stylistically polished speeches; the philosopher has no patience for the "long style of speech," insisting instead on "discussion," a dialogue in which the participants join together to seek the truth by critically examining one another's views (e.g., 449b–c). As Plato draws the contrast, this external difference is symptomatic of a much more fundamental difference in aims, values, and methods.

In the discussion with Gorgias Socrates is treated to a panegyric on behalf of oratory. Oratory enables its practitioner "to rule over others in his own city" (452d), because it furnishes him with "the ability to persuade" (452e) various sorts of political audiences, without requiring him to have expertise in the subjects about which he speaks. The orator has in fact the ability to speak more persuasively than experts on a technical matter before a crowd of nonexperts (456a–c; 458e–9c). Since he produces "conviction-persuasion" and not "teaching-persuasion" (455a), the orator is required neither to know nor to speak the truth about the matters of which he speaks, and hence can easily afford to be indifferent to the truth. Under Socrates' questioning Gorgias declares that the orator produces persuasion about "matters that are just and unjust" (454b). If the orator can be indifferent to truth, can he be indifferent to justice? Here Gorgias' portrait of the orator shows some uncertainty. On the one hand, he maintains that the orator does not need to know what is just in order to persuade an audience that a given course of action is just. The orator's recommendation of it as just may reflect no more than his own self-interest (452e). On the other hand, Gorgias is concerned about the fact that oratory can be used unjustly, that is, in a way contrary to the interest of those whom, like one's parents, relatives, and friends, one has an obligation not to harm (456c – 57c). Clearly disapproving of such a use, and prompted by Socrates' questioning, Gorgias agrees that the prospective orator should learn (and hence know) what is just before beginning practice.

By conceding that a knowledge of what is just is a prerequisite for practicing oratory, Gorgias indicates that ordinary considerations of what is just ought to restrain the practice of oratory. Seeing clearly that this concession undermines Gorgias's own panegyric of oratory, Polus, his successor in the discussion, disavows any such restraint. He endorses Gorgias's conception of the orator as one who has power over others and identifies this power as that of being in the position of doing whatever he sees fit in his city (466c – e). Here we begin to see that oratory is connected with a way of life. If the value of oratory lies in the opportunity it provides for the use of unrestrained political power, then a career or life in which such power is exercised is itself to be desired. Such a life is desirable because it is the happy *(eudaimon)* life (see n. 1). To allow the use of this power to be restrained by considerations of what is just is to surrender one's prospects for happiness. Polus's vivid description of the tyrant Archelaus advertises a life of unjust action as better, more advantageous, and therefore happier than a life limited by justice; although he concedes that doing what is unjust is more shameful than suffering it, he insists that the former is by far the better.

It is in Socrates' conversation with Polus that the philosophical way of life begins to emerge as a foil to that of the orator-politician. Here again we find a contrast between the philosopher's and the orator's mode of discussion. Polus thinks that he refutes Socrates both by denouncing his views as outrageous and by appealing to the support of popular opinion for his own views. Socrates, repudiating that "method of refutation," recalls him to argumentation. Moreover, Socrates, who is not only the protagonist for the philosophic way of life but also its incarnation, assumes a new, and uncharacteristic, role in this part of the dialogue. During the earlier discussion with Gorgias, Socrates had played his usual role, familiar from most of Plato's other early dialogues,[2] as questioner. His customary use of the *elenchus*[3] to examine the views of his interlocutors without introducing or defending his own views was apparent there. Early in the discussion with Polus, however, when he is asked point blank what he thinks of oratory, Socrates is uncharacteristically forthcoming with his own views. Furthermore, he introduces them with an earnestness that grows in intensity as the dialogue progresses. When he later resumes the use of the *elenchus*, he is as much defending or "proving" his own views as refuting their contradictories, affirmed first by Polus and then by Callicles (479e; 508e – 509a). Although his customary disclaimer to have knowledge of these matters remains formally intact (506a; 509a) and his readiness to reexamine his own convictions is as much in evidence as ever (458a,b; 506a), he is morally certain not only that *his* beliefs about the issues in dispute are the true ones and those of his interlocutors the false ones but also that the *elenchus* will always show them to be so (473b).[4] Consequently, the positions that Socrates defends, the contradictories of those which Polus

[2]The *Gorgias* is generally considered to be one of the last of Plato's early dialogues and so is often thought to represent the views, methods, and personality of the historical Socrates. See W. K. C. Guthrie, *A History of Greek Philosophy*, 3:325 – 77, and 4:39 – 66; 284 – 312.

[3]The name generally given to Socrates' method of refutation in the early dialogues. For an important recent discussion of it, see Vlastos and Kraut in *Oxford Studies in Ancient Philosophy*, ed, J. Annas (Oxford: 1983), 1: 27 – 74.

[4]On the problem of Socrates' disclaimer to have knowledge, see Vlastos, "Socrates' Disavowal of Knowledge," *Philosophical Quarterly* 35 (1985): 1 – 31.

takes to define the conception of happiness which he embraces, will be equally definitive of the philosophic life and its conception of happiness.

Polus had agreed that suffering what is unjust is less shameful than doing it, but had denied that it is better. Having been shown by several arguments that if suffering what is unjust is less shameful, it is also less bad, Polus is reduced to silence (but not to consent) and retires from the discussion. His part is taken up by Callicles, who denies what Polus had admitted: that suffering what is unjust is less shameful than doing it. This may be so "by law," but it is not so "by nature" (see 482 and the note there). Since nature and not law is what we should follow, the argument from the claim that doing what is unjust is more shameful than suffering it, to the claim that it is therefore also more evil, will not serve to establish that it is in fact more evil. Callicles asserts that, judged by the standard of nature, unjust action is not only better, but also more admirable than suffering what is unjust (483a – c). He recommends as just (by nature) a state of affairs in which those who are superior "have a greater share" than their inferiors. He goes on to denounce the philosophical life as lacking in all the resources and accomplishments necessary for survival, let alone success, in the public arena (484c – 86d). It is Callicles, then, who first explicitly introduces the philosophic way of life in contrast to that of the orator-politician. Moreover, he is the first to exhort his interlocutor to make the right choice between them. He contemptuously denies that the superior individual, whom he identifies as one who exercises political rule (491c – d), "rules himself," that is, restrains his pleasures and appetites; on the contrary, such a person devotes his courage and his intelligence to maximizing his capacity for them. Can such a life qualify as a happy one? After offering some striking images intended to represent the futility of a life that makes the experience of pleasure and the satisfaction of appetites its end—images failing to persuade Callicles—Socrates undertakes a refutation of hedonism, the view that pleasure is to be identified with goodness. Callicles admits that some pleasures are better and others worse, thereby admitting that there is a standard of goodness distinct from pleasure, by which pleasures are to be evaluated. This admission is crucial: it justifies Socrates' earlier distinction between practices that aim at producing what is pleasant and those that aim at producing what is good. Socrates links the practices so distinguished to the two different lives that he and Callicles represent and advocate (500b – d) and proposes an investigation into these two lives. The orator-politician is described as a person who engages in one of the practices that aim at producing pleasure without any regard for what is good. Socrates allows no exception for the great Athenian statesmen of the past; they, too, pandered to the pleasures of their charges, without taking thought for their good, as the results of their political careers show (503c – d; 515d – 16e). A true craftsman considers the good of the craft's subject, and this good is described in terms of order and organization (503e – 504b). This principle is equally true when the subject of the craft is the soul: a true craftsman of souls will strive to make souls orderly and well organized by rendering them just and self-controlled and ridding them of injustice and indiscipline. Persons whose souls are thus made good will be happy; those whose souls are unjust and undisciplined will be miserable (507c). The principles of order and organization that determine the goodness of one's soul are the very principles that underlie the world-order, and are thus cosmic in scope (508a).

Socrates' appeal to cosmic order as the basis of psychic goodness is one that he does not attempt to justify, and so it may be taken as a foundational principle for the philosophical life. If those characteristics that "hold together heaven and earth, and gods and men" (508a) define the excellence of one's soul, they thereby determine the kind of life one ought to live. The maintenance and promotion of that excellence will be definitive of the happy life. A craft is needed that will equip a person to maintain and promote that excellence of soul (509c – 10a). This craft is the "true political craft," and Socrates claims to be one of a very few Athenians who have practiced it (521d). The "true politician" not only knows what is good and bad for the soul, but also strives to make souls (his own and those of others) good, a task at which the past as well as the present Athenian politicians have failed decisively.

The contrast between the two lives is continued in the eschatological myth which closes the dialogue (523a–27e). Socrates declares that the narrative he there presents is an "account" *(logos)*, and not a mere "tale" *(muthos)* and affirms the truth of the account (523a). The precise meaning of this claim is hard to determine. Nevertheless, it is clear that Socrates is prepared to acknowledge not only that the consequences of the choice of life one makes are not limited to one's earthly existence but also that those further consequences provide part of a justification for choosing the life of the philosopher and the "true politician" over that of the orator-politician. The myth is undoubtedly an integral, if not an indispensable, part of Socrates' case against the life that Callicles represents and that he urges Socrates to take up.

The *Gorgias* shows Plato raising some fundamental questions of ethics: What is wrong with the unrestrained use of power? How is the happy human life to be determined? Why is justice better than injustice? What is wrong with a life of unrestrained self-gratification? All these questions are summed up by Socrates' statement, "Our discussion is about the way we're supposed to live" (500c). The answers Plato gives here are not his final answers to these questions. He will return to these questions in the *Republic;* with a more developed metaphysics and psychology, he will answer them afresh.

The Text

I have based my translation primarily on Dodds's text (Oxford, 1959), occasionally preferring Burnet's text (Oxford Classical Texts, 1903).

Selected Bibliography

Books

Adkins, A. W. H. *Merit and Responsibility*. Oxford: Clarendon Press, 1960.

———. *Moral Value and Political Behaviour in Ancient Greece*. New York: Norton, 1972.

Burnet, J. *Platonis Opera*, vol. 3. Oxford Classical Texts. Oxford: Clarendon Press, 1903.

Crombie, I. M. *An Examination of Plato's Doctrines*, vol. 1. London: Routledge and Kegan Paul, 1962.

Dilman, I. *Morality and Inner Life: A Study in Plato's Gorgias*. Totowa, N.J.: Barnes and Noble, 1979.

Dodds, E. R. *Plato: Gorgias*, text and commentary. Oxford: Clarendon Press, 1959.

Dover, K. J. *Greek Popular Morality in the Time of Plato and Aristotle*. Oxford: Blackwell, 1974.

Gosling, J. C. B. *Plato*. London: Routledge and Kegan Paul, 1973.

———, and C. C. W. Taylor. *The Greeks on Pleasure*. Oxford: Oxford University Press, 1982.

Gulley, N. *The Philosophy of Socrates*. London: Macmillan, 1968.

Guthrie, W. K. C. *The Fifth Century Enlightenment*. Vol. 3 of *A History of Greek Philosophy*. Cambridge: Cambridge University Press, 1969. (Also available in two volumes, *The Sophists* and *Socrates*, 1971.)

———. *Plato, the Man and His Dialogues, Earlier Period*. Vol. 4 of *A History of Greek Philosophy*. Cambridge: Cambridge University Press, 1975.

Irwin. T. H. *Plato: Gorgias*, translation and commentary. Oxford: Clarendon Press, 1979.

———. *Plato's Moral Theory: The Early and Middle Dialogues.* Oxford: Clarendon Press, 1977.

Kerferd, G. B. *The Sophistic Movement.* Cambridge: Cambridge University Press, 1981.

Plochmann, G. K. and Franklin E. Robinson. *A Friendly Companion to Plato's* Gorgias. Carbondale and Edwardsville: Southern Illinois University Press, 1987.

Robinson, R. *Plato's Earlier Dialectic,* 2d ed. Oxford: Clarendon Press, 1953.

Santas, G. *Socrates.* London: Routledge and Kegan Paul, 1979.

Vlastos, G., ed. *The Philosophy of Socrates.* New York: Doubleday, 1971.

———, ed. *Plato,* vol. 2. New York: Doubleday, 1971.

———. *Platonic Studies,* 2d ed. Princeton, N.J.: Princeton University Press, 1981.

Articles

Annas, J. "Plato's Myths of Judgement." *Phronesis* 27 (1982): 119 – 43.

Anton, John P. "Dialectic and Health in Plato's Gorgias." *Ancient Philosophy* 1 (1980): 49 – 60.

Hall, R. W. "Technē and Morality in the Gorgias." In *Essays in Ancient Greek Philosophy,* pp. 202 – 18. Ed. John P. Anton and George L. Kustas. Albany, N.Y.: SUNY Press, 1971.

Kahn, C. H. "Drama and Dialectic in Plato's Gorgias." In *Oxford Studies in Ancient Philosophy,* vol. 1, pp. 75 – 121. Ed. J. Annas. Oxford: Clarendon Press, 1983.

Kerferd, G. B. "Plato's Treatment of Callicles in the Gorgias." *Proceedings of the Cambridge Philological Society* 20 (1974): 48 – 52.

Kraut, R. "Comments on Gregory Vlastos, 'The Socratic Elenchus.' " In *Oxford Studies in Ancient Philosophy,* vol. 1, pp. 59 – 70. Ed. J. Annas. Oxford: Clarendon Press, 1983.

Santas, G. "The Socratic Paradox." *Philosophical Review* 73 (1964): 147 – 64.

Vlastos, G. "Was Polus Refuted?" *American Journal of Philology* 88 (1967): 454 – 60.

———. "The Socratic Elenchus" and "Afterthoughts on the Socratic Elenchus." In *Oxford Studies in Ancient Philosophy*, 27 – 58, 71 – 74. vol. 1, Ed. J. Annas. Oxford: Clarendon Press, 1983.

———. "Socrates' Disavowal of Knowledge." *Philosophical Quarterly* 35 (1985): 1 – 31.

———. "Happiness and Virtue in Socrates' Moral Theory." *Proceedings of the Cambridge Philological Society*, n.s. 30 (1984): 181 – 213.

Zeyl, D. J. "Socratic Virtue and Happiness." *Archiv fuer Geschichte der Philosophie* 64 (1982): 225 – 38.

GORGIAS

CALLICLES SOCRATES CHAEREPHON

GORGIAS POLUS

CALLICLES: This, they say, is how you're supposed to do your part in a war or a battle, Socrates. 447a

SOCRATES: Oh? Did we "arrive when the feast was over," as the saying goes? Are we late?[1]

CALLICLES: Yes, and a very urbane one it was! Gorgias gave us an admirable, varied presentation[2] just a short while ago.

SOCRATES: But that's Chaerephon's fault, Callicles. He kept us loitering about in the marketplace.

CHAEREPHON: That's no problem, Socrates. I'll make up b
for it, too. Gorgias is a friend of mine, so he'll give us a presentation—now, if you see fit, or else some other time, if you like.

CALLICLES: What's this, Chaerephon? Is Socrates eager to hear Gorgias?

[1]The setting of the dialogue is not clear. We may suppose that the conversation takes place outside a public building in Athens such as the gymnasium (see the reference to persons "inside" at 447c and 455c).

In the exchange that opens the dialogue, Callicles and Socrates are evidently alluding to a Greek saying, unknown to us, the equivalent of the English phrase, "first at a feast, last at a fray." Cf. Shakespeare, *Henry IV, Part 1*, Act 4, Sc. 2.

[2]Gr. *epideiknusthai*. An *epideixis* was a lecture regularly given by sophists as a public display of their oratorical prowess.

CHAEREPHON: Yes. That's the very thing we're here for.

CALLICLES: Well then, come to my house any time you like. Gorgias is staying with me and will give you a presentation there.

SOCRATES: Very good, Callicles. But would he be willing
c to have a discussion[3] with us? I'd like to find out from the man what his craft[4] can accomplish, and what it is that he both makes claims about and teaches. As for the other thing, the presentation, let him put that on another time, as you suggest.

CALLICLES: There's nothing like asking him, Socrates. This was, in fact, one part of his presentation. Just now he invited those inside to ask him any question they liked, and he said that he'd answer them all.

SOCRATES: An excellent idea. Ask him, Chaerephon.

CHAEREPHON: Ask him what?

d SOCRATES: What he is.

CHAEREPHON: What do you mean?

SOCRATES: Well, if he were a maker of shoes, he'd answer that he was a cobbler, wouldn't he? Or don't you see what I mean?

CHAEREPHON: I do. I'll ask him. Tell me, Gorgias, is Callicles right in saying that you make claims about answering any question anyone might put to you?

448a GORGIAS: He is, Chaerephon. In fact I just now made that very claim, and I say that no one has asked me anything new in many a year.

[3]Gr. *dialegesthai.* Socrates already here indicates his aversion to monologues. See 449b,c; 461d; 465e, and elsewhere. He favors dialogue, the method of "alternately asking questions and answering them" (449b). The contrast between orator and philosopher, a major theme of this dialogue, includes a contrast in style of speech.

[4]Gr. *technē.* Socrates uses this term deferentially here. He will go on to deny that oratory is a craft (462c), but at this point Gorgias's occupation has not yet been identified. Socrates' conditions for any enterprise being a *technē* include the following: (1) a *technē* is a rational enterprise, the procedures of which can be explained as contributing to an end (see 465a); and (2) a practitioner of a *technē* aims to produce some good (see 500b).

CHAEREPHON: In that case I'm sure you'll answer this one quite easily, Gorgias.

GORGIAS: Here's your chance to try me, Chaerephon.

POLUS: By Zeus, Chaerephon! Try me, if you like! I think Gorgias is quite worn out. He's only just now finished a long discourse.

CHAEREPHON: Really, Polus? Do you think you'd give more admirable answers than Gorgias?

POLUS: What does it matter, as long as they're good b
enough for you?

CHAEREPHON: Nothing at all! You answer us then, since that's what you want.

POLUS: Ask your questions.

CHAEREPHON: I will. Suppose that Gorgias were an expert in his brother Herodicus's craft. What would be the right name for us to call him by then? Isn't it the same one as his brother's?

POLUS: Yes, it is.

CHAEREPHON: So we'd be right in saying that he's a doctor?

POLUS: Yes.

CHAEREPHON: And if he were experienced in the craft of Aristophon the son of Aglaophon or his brother, what would be the correct thing to call him?

POLUS: A painter, obviously. c

CHAEREPHON: Now then, since he's an expert in a craft, what is it, and what would be the correct thing to call him?

POLUS: Many among men are the crafts devised by experience, Chaerephon, the results of experience. Yes, it is experience that causes our times to march along the way of craft, whereas inexperience causes it to march along the way of chance. Of these various crafts various men partake in various ways, the best men partaking of the best of them. Our Gorgias is indeed in this group; he partakes of the most admirable of the crafts.[5]

[5]This bit of oratorical flourish may be in part a quotation from one of Polus's published speeches (see 462b), or, perhaps more likely, a Platonic parody of the Gorgian oratorical style.

d SOCRATES: Polus certainly appears to have prepared himself admirably for giving speeches, Gorgias. But he's not doing what he promised Chaerephon.

GORGIAS: How exactly isn't he, Socrates?

SOCRATES: He hardly seems to me to be answering the question.

GORGIAS: Why don't you question him then, if you like?

SOCRATES: No, I won't, not as long as you yourself may want to answer. I'd much rather ask you. It's clear to me, especially from what he has said, that Polus has devoted himself more to what is called oratory than to discussing.

e POLUS: Why do you say that, Socrates?

SOCRATES: Because, Polus, when Chaerephon asks you what craft Gorgias is knowledgeable in, you sing its praises as though someone were discrediting it. But you haven't answered what it is.

POLUS: Didn't I answer that it was the most admirable one?

SOCRATES: Very much so. No one, however, asked you what Gorgias's craft is like, but what craft it is, and what one ought to call Gorgias. So, just as when Chaerephon put his
449a earlier questions to you and you answered him in such an admirably brief way, tell us now in that way, too, what his craft is, and what we're supposed to call Gorgias. Or rather, Gorgias, why don't you tell us yourself what the craft you're an expert in is, and hence what we're supposed to call you?

GORGIAS: It's oratory, Socrates.[6]

SOCRATES: So we're supposed to call you an orator?

GORGIAS: Yes, and a good one, Socrates, if you really want to call me "what I boast myself to be," as Homer puts it.[7]

SOCRATES: Of course I do.

GORGIAS: Call me that then.

b SOCRATES: Aren't we to say that you're capable of making others orators too?

[6]Gr. *rhētorikē*; see introduction.

[7]*Iliad* 6. 211.

GORGIAS: That's exactly the claim I make. Not only here, but elsewhere, too.

SOCRATES: Well now, Gorgias, would you be willing to complete the discussion in the way we're having it right now, that of alternately asking questions and answering them, and to put aside for another time this long style of speechmaking like the one Polus began with? Please don't go back on your promise, but be willing to give a brief answer to what you're asked.

GORGIAS: There are some answers, Socrates, that must be given by way of long speeches. Even so, I'll try to be as brief c
as possible. This, too, in fact, is one of my claims. There's no one who can say the same things more briefly than I.

SOCRATES: That's what we need, Gorgias! Do give me a presentation of this very thing, the short style of speech, and leave the long style for some other time.

GORGIAS: Very well, I'll do that. You'll say you've never heard anyone make shorter speeches.

SOCRATES: Come then. You claim to be an expert in the
craft of oratory and to be able to make someone else an orator, d
too. With which of the things there are is oratory concerned? Weaving, for example, is concerned with the production of clothes, isn't it?

GORGIAS: Yes.

SOCRATES: And so, too, music is concerned with the composition of tunes?

GORGIAS: Yes.

SOCRATES: By Hera, Gorgias, I do like your answers. They couldn't be shorter!

GORGIAS: Yes, Socrates, I daresay I'm doing it quite nicely.

SOCRATES: And so you are. Come and answer me then that way about oratory, too. About which, of the things there are, is *it* expertise?

GORGIAS: About speeches. e

SOCRATES: What sort of speeches, Gorgias? Those that explain how sick people should be treated to get well?

GORGIAS: No.

SOCRATES: So oratory isn't concerned with *all* speeches.

GORGIAS: Oh, no.

SOCRATES: But it does make people capable of speaking.

GORGIAS: Yes.

SOCRATES: And also to be wise in what they're speaking about?

GORGIAS: Of course.

450a SOCRATES: Now does the medical craft, the one we were talking about just now, make people able both to have wisdom about and to speak about the sick?

GORGIAS: Necessarily.

SOCRATES: This craft, then, is evidently concerned with speeches too.

GORGIAS: Yes.

SOCRATES: Speeches about diseases, that is?

GORGIAS: Exactly.

SOCRATES: Isn't physical training also concerned with speeches, speeches about good and bad physical condition?

GORGIAS: Yes, it is.

SOCRATES: In fact, Gorgias, the same is true of the other
b crafts, too. Each of them is concerned with those speeches that are about the object of the particular craft.

GORGIAS: Apparently.

SOCRATES: Then why don't you call the other crafts oratory, since you call any craft whatever that's concerned with speeches oratory? They're concerned with speeches, too!

GORGIAS: The reason, Socrates, is that in the case of the other crafts the expertise consists almost completely in working with your hands and activities of that sort. In the case of oratory, on the other hand, there isn't any such manual work. Its activity and influence depend entirely on speeches. That's
c the reason I consider the craft of oratory to be concerned with speeches. And I say that I'm right about this.

SOCRATES: I'm not sure I understand what sort of craft you want to call it. I'll soon know more clearly. Tell me this. There are crafts at our disposal, aren't there?

GORGIAS: Yes.

SOCRATES: Of all the crafts there are, I take it that there
are those that consist for the most part of making things and
that call for little speech, and some that call for none at all,
ones whose task could be done even silently. Take painting, for
instance, or sculpture, or many others. When you say that oratory has nothing to do with other crafts, it's crafts of this sort I d
think you're referring to. Or aren't you?

GORGIAS: Yes, Socrates. You take my meaning very well.

SOCRATES: And then there are other crafts, the ones that
perform their whole task by means of speeches and that call
for practically no physical work besides, or very little of it.
Take arithmetic or computation or geometry, even checkers
and many other crafts. Some of these involve speeches to just
about the same degree as they do activity, while others involve
speeches more. All their activity and influence depend entirely on speeches. I think you mean that oratory is a craft of e
this sort.

GORGIAS: True.

SOCRATES: But you certainly don't want to call any of *these* crafts oratory, do you, even though, as you phrase it, oratory is the craft that exercises its influence through speech. Somebody might take you up, if he wanted to make a fuss in argument, and say, "So you're saying that arithmetic is oratory, are you, Gorgias?" I'm sure, however, that you're not saying that either arithmetic or geometry is oratory.

GORGIAS: Yes, you're quite correct, Socrates. You take my 451a
meaning rightly.

SOCRATES: Come on, then. Please complete your answer
in the terms of my question. Since oratory is one of those crafts
which mostly uses speech, and since there are also others of
that sort, try to say *what* it is that oratory, which exercises its
influence through speeches, is about. Imagine someone asking
me about any of the crafts I mentioned just now, "Socrates,
what is the craft of arithmetic?" I'd tell him, just as you told b
me, that it's one of those that exercise their influence by means
of speech. And if he continued, "What are they crafts about?"
I'd say that they're about even and odd, however many of each

there might be. If he then asked, "What is the craft you call
computation?" I'd say that this one, too, is one of those that
exercise their influence entirely by speech. And if he then
continued, "What is it about?" I'd answer in the style of those
c who draw up motions in the Assembly that in other respects
computation is like arithmetic—for it's about the same thing,
even and odd—yet it differs from arithmetic insofar as computation examines the quantity of odd and even, both in relation to themselves and in relation to each other. And if someone asked about astronomy and I replied that it, too, exercises
its influence by means of speech, then if he asked, "What are
the speeches of astronomy about, Socrates?" I'd say that they're
about the motions of the stars, the sun and the moon, and
their relative velocities.

GORGIAS: And you'd be quite right to say so, Socrates.

d SOCRATES: Come, Gorgias, you take your turn. For oratory is in fact one of those crafts that carry out and exercise
their influence entirely by speech, isn't it?

GORGIAS: That's right.

SOCRATES: Tell us then: what are they crafts about? Of the things there are, which is the one that these speeches used by oratory are concerned with?

GORGIAS: The greatest of human concerns, Socrates, and the best.

SOCRATES: But that statement, too, is debatable, Gorgias.
e It isn't at all clear yet, either. I'm sure that you've heard people
at drinking parties singing that song in which they count out
as they sing that "to enjoy good health is the best thing; second
is to have turned out good looking; and third"—so the writer
of the song puts it—"is to be honestly rich."

GORGIAS: Yes, I've heard it. Why do you mention it?

452a SOCRATES: Suppose that the producers of the things the
songwriter praised were here with you right now: a doctor, a
physical trainer, and a financial expert. Suppose that first the
doctor said, "Socrates, Gorgias is telling you a lie. It isn't his
craft that is concerned with the greatest good for mankind, but
mine." If I then asked him, "What are you, to say that?" I
suppose he'd say that he's a doctor. "What's this you're saying? Is

the product of *your* craft really the greatest good?" "Of course, Socrates," I suppose he'd say, "seeing that its product is health.
What greater good for mankind is there than health?" And b
suppose that next in his turn the trainer said, "I too would be amazed, Socrates, if Gorgias could present you with a greater good derived from his craft than the one I could provide from mine." I'd ask this man, too, "What are you, sir, and what's your product?" "I'm a physical trainer," he'd say, "and my product is making people physically good-looking and strong." And following the trainer the financial expert would say, I'm sure with
an air of considerable scorn for all, "Do consider, Socrates, c
whether you know of any good, Gorgias's or anyone else's, that's a greater good than wealth." We'd say to him, "Really? Is that what you produce?" He'd say yes. "As what?" "As a financial expert." "Well," we'll say, "is wealth in your judgment the greatest good for humankind?" "Of course," he'll say. "Ah, but Gorgias here disputes that. He claims that his craft is the source of a good that's greater than yours," we'd say. And it's obvious what question he'd ask next. "And what is this good,
please? Let Gorgias answer me that!" So come on, Gorgias. d
Consider yourself questioned by both these men and myself, and give us your answer. What is this thing that you claim is the greatest good for mankind, a thing you claim to be a producer of?

GORGIAS: The thing that is in actual fact the greatest good, Socrates. It is the source of freedom for mankind itself and at the same time it is for each person the source of rule over others in one's own city.

SOCRATES: And what is this thing you're referring to?

GORGIAS: I'm referring to the ability to persuade by e
speeches judges in a law court, councillors in a council meeting, and assemblymen in an assembly or in any other political gathering that might take place. In point of fact, with this ability you'll have the doctor for your slave, and the physical trainer, too. As for this financial expert of yours, he'll turn out to be making more money for somebody else instead of himself; for you, in fact, if you've got the ability to speak and to persuade the crowds.

SOCRATES: *Now* I think you've come closest to making
453a clear what craft you take oratory to be, Gorgias. If I follow you at all, you're saying that oratory is a producer of persuasion. Its whole business comes to that, and that's the long and short of it. Or can you mention anything else oratory can do besides instilling persuasion in the souls of an audience?

GORGIAS: None at all, Socrates. I think you're defining it quite adequately. That is indeed the long and short of it.

SOCRATES: Listen then, Gorgias. You should know that
b I'm convinced I'm one of those people who in a discussion with someone else really want to have knowledge of the subject the discussion's about. And I consider you one of them, too.

GORGIAS: Well, what's the point, Socrates?

SOCRATES: Let me tell you now. You can know for sure that I don't know what this persuasion derived from oratory that you're talking about is, or what subjects it's persuasion about. Even though I do have my suspicions about which persuasion I think you mean, and what it's about, I'll still ask you just the same what you say this persuasion produced by
c oratory is, and what it's about. And why, when I have my suspicions, do I ask you and refrain from expressing them myself? It's not you I'm after, it's our discussion, to have it proceed in such a way as to make the thing we're talking about most clear to us. Consider, then, whether you think I'm being fair in resuming my questions to you. Suppose I were to ask you which of the painters Zeuxis is.[8] If you told me that he's the one who paints pictures, wouldn't it be fair for me to ask, "Of what sort of pictures is he the painter, and where?"

GORGIAS: Yes, it would.

d SOCRATES: And isn't the reason for this the fact that there are other painters, too, who paint many other pictures?

GORGIAS: Yes.

SOCRATES: But if no one besides Zeuxis were a painter, your answer would have been a good one?

GORGIAS: Of course.

[8]Zeuxis was the most famous painter of the late fifth century.

SOCRATES: Come then, and tell me about oratory. Do you think that oratory alone instills persuasion, or do other crafts do so too? This is the sort of thing I mean: Does a person who teaches some subject or other persuade people about what he's teaching, or not?

GORGIAS: He certainly does, Socrates. He persuades most of all.

SOCRATES: Let's talk once more about the same crafts we e were talking about just now. Doesn't arithmetic or the arithmetician teach us everything that pertains to number?

GORGIAS: Yes, he does.

SOCRATES: And he also persuades?

GORGIAS: Yes.

SOCRATES: So arithmetic is also a producer of persuasion.

GORGIAS: Apparently.

SOCRATES: Now if someone asks us what sort of persuasion it produces and what it's persuasion about, I suppose we'd answer him that it's the persuasion of teaching about the extent of even and odd. And we'll be able to show that all the other 454a crafts we were just now talking about are producers of persuasion, as well as what the persuasion is and what it's about. Isn't that right?

GORGIAS: Yes.

SOCRATES: So oratory isn't the only producer of persuasion.

GORGIAS: That's true.

SOCRATES: In that case, since it's not the only one to produce this product but other crafts do it too, we'd do right to repeat to our speaker the question we put next in the case of the painter: "Of what sort of persuasion is oratory a craft, and what is its persuasion about?" Or don't you think it's right to repeat that question? b

GORGIAS: Yes, I do.

SOCRATES: Well then, Gorgias, since you think so too, please answer.

GORGIAS: The persuasion I mean, Socrates, is the kind that takes place in law courts and in those other large gatherings, as I was saying a moment ago. And it's concerned with those matters that are just and unjust.

SOCRATES: Yes, Gorgias, I suspected that this was the persuasion you meant, and that these are the matters it's persuasion about. But so you won't be surprised if in a moment I ask you again another question like this, about what seems to
c be clear, and yet I go on with my questioning—as I say, I'm asking questions so that we can conduct an orderly discussion. It's not you I'm after; it's to prevent our getting in the habit of second-guessing and snatching each other's statements away ahead of time. It's to allow you to work out your assumption in any way you want to.

GORGIAS: Yes, I think that you're quite right to do this, Socrates.

SOCRATES: Come then, and let's examine this point. Is there something you call "to have learned"?

GORGIAS: There is.

SOCRATES: Very well. And also something you call "to be convinced"?

d GORGIAS: Yes, there is.

SOCRATES: Now, do you think that to have learned, and learning, are the same as to be convinced and conviction, or different?

GORGIAS: I certainly suppose that they're different, Socrates.

SOCRATES: You suppose rightly. This is how you can tell: If someone asked you, "Is there such a thing as true and false conviction, Gorgias?" you'd say yes, I'm sure.

GORGIAS: Yes.

SOCRATES: Well now, is there such a thing as true and false knowledge?

GORGIAS: Not at all.

SOCRATES: So it's clear that they're not the same.

GORGIAS: That's true.

e SOCRATES: But surely both those who have learned and those who are convinced have come to be persuaded?

GORGIAS: That's right.

SOCRATES: Would you like us then to posit two types of persuasion, one providing conviction without knowledge, the other providing knowledge?

GORGIAS: Yes, I would.

SOCRATES: Now which type of persuasion does oratory produce in law courts and other gatherings concerning things that are just and unjust? The one that results in being convinced without knowing or the one that results in knowing?

GORGIAS: It's obvious, surely, that it's the one that results in conviction.

SOCRATES: So evidently oratory is a producer of conviction-persuasion and not of teaching-persuasion concerning 455a
what's just and unjust.

GORGIAS: Yes.

SOCRATES: And so an orator is not a teacher of law courts and other gatherings about things that are just and unjust, either, but merely a persuader, for I don't suppose that he could teach such a large gathering about matters so important in a short time.

GORGIAS: No, he certainly couldn't.

SOCRATES: Well now, let's see what we're really saying
about oratory. For, mind you, even I myself can't get clear yet b
about what I'm saying. When the city holds a meeting to appoint doctors or shipbuilders or some other variety of craftsmen, that's surely not the time when the orator will give advice, is it? For obviously it's the most accomplished craftsman who should be appointed in each case. Nor will the orator be the one to give advice at a meeting that concerns the building of walls or the equipping of harbors or dockyards, but the master builders will be the ones. And when there is a deliberation about the appointment of generals or an arrangement of
troops against the enemy or an occupation of territory, it's not c
the orators but the generals who'll give advice then. What do you say about such cases, Gorgias? Since you yourself claim both to be an orator and to make others orators, we'll do well to find out from you the characteristics of your craft. You must think of me now as eager to serve your interests, too. Perhaps there's actually someone inside who wants to become your pupil. I notice some, in fact a good many, and they may well be embarrassed to question you. So, while you're being questioned
by me, consider yourself being questioned by them as well: d

"What will we get if we associate with you, Gorgias? What will we be able to advise the city on? Only about what's just and unjust or also about the things Socrates was mentioning just now?" Try to answer them.

GORGIAS: Well, Socrates, I'll try to reveal to you clearly everything oratory can accomplish. You yourself led the way nicely, for you do know, don't you, that these dockyards
e and walls of the Athenians and the equipping of the harbor came about through the advice of Themistocles and in some cases through that of Pericles, but not through that of the craftsmen?[9]

SOCRATES: That's what they say about Themistocles, Gorgias. I myself heard Pericles when he advised us on the middle wall.

456a GORGIAS: And whenever those craftsmen you were just now speaking of are appointed, Socrates, you see that the orators are the ones who give advice and whose views on these matters prevail.

SOCRATES: Yes, Gorgias, my amazement at that led me long ago to ask what it is that oratory can accomplish. For as I look at it, it seems to me to be something supernatural in scope.

GORGIAS: Oh yes, Socrates, if only you knew all of it, that it encompasses and subordinates to itself just about every-
b thing that can be accomplished. And I'll give you ample proof. Many a time I've gone with my brother or with other doctors to call on some sick person who refuses to take his medicine or allow the doctor to perform surgery or cauterization on him. And when the doctor failed to persuade him, I succeeded, by

[9]Themistocles (c. 528 – c. 462 B.C.) was the leading statesman of Athens after the death of Miltiades in 489. He was largely responsible for the fortification of the Piraeus, and for the development of Athens's naval power during the first two decades of the fifth century. Pericles (c. 495 – 429 B.C.) rose to prominence in the late 460s, and in 443 and every year of his life thereafter was elected as general. He was the architect of Athenian strategy against Sparta at the outbreak of the Peloponnesian war in 431. He died in 429 from the effects of the plague that had struck Athens a year earlier.

means of no other craft than oratory. And I maintain too that if
an orator and a doctor came to any city anywhere you like and
had to compete in speaking in the assembly or some other
gathering over which of them should be appointed doctor, the
doctor wouldn't make any showing at all, but the one who had c
the ability to speak would be appointed, if he so wished. And
if he were to compete with any other craftsman whatever, the
orator more than anyone else would persuade them that they
should appoint him, for there isn't anything that the orator
couldn't speak more persuasively about to a gathering than
could any other craftsman whatever. That's how great the accomplishment of this craft is, and the sort of accomplishment
it is! One should, however, use oratory like any other competitive skill, Socrates. In other cases, too, one ought not to use a d
competitive skill against any and everybody, just because he
has learned boxing, or boxing and wrestling combined, or
fighting in armor, so as to make himself be superior to his
friends as well as to his enemies. That's no reason to strike,
stab, or kill one's own friends! Imagine someone who after
attending wrestling school, getting his body into good shape
and becoming a boxer, went on to strike his father and mother
or any other family member or friend. By Zeus, that's no reason
to hate physical trainers and people who teach fighting in e
armor, and to exile them from their cities! For while these
people imparted their skills to be used justly against enemies
and wrongdoers, and in defense, not aggression, their pupils
pervert their strength and skill and misuse them. So it's not 457a
their teachers who are wicked, nor is this a reason why the
craft should be a cause of wickedness; the ones who misuse it
are supposedly the wicked ones. And the same is true for
oratory as well. The orator has the ability to speak against
everyone on every subject, so as in gatherings to be more persuasive, in short, about anything he likes, but the fact that he b
has the ability to rob doctors or other craftsmen of their repu-
tations doesn't give him any more of a reason to do it. He
should use oratory justly, as he would any competitive skill.
And I suppose that if a person who has become an orator goes
on with this ability and this craft to commit wrongdoing, we

shouldn't hate his teacher and exile him from our cities. For
c while the teacher imparted it to be used justly, the pupil is
making the opposite use of it. So it's the misuser whom it's just
to hate and exile or put to death, not the teacher.

SOCRATES: Gorgias, I take it that you, like me, have experienced many discussions and that you've observed this sort of
thing about them: it's not easy for the participants to define
jointly what they're undertaking to discuss, and so, having
d learned from and taught each other, to conclude their session.
Instead, if they're disputing some point and one maintains that
the other isn't right or isn't clear, they get irritated, each thinking the other is speaking out of spite. They become eager to
win instead of investigating the subject under discussion. In
fact, in the end some have a most shameful parting of the ways,
abuse heaped upon them, having given and gotten to hear such
things that make even the bystanders upset with themselves for
having thought it worthwhile to come to listen to such people.
e What's my point in saying this? It's that I think you're now
saying things that aren't very consistent or compatible with
what you were first saying about oratory. So, I'm afraid to pursue my examination of you, for fear that you should take me to
be speaking with eagerness to win against you, rather than to
458a have our subject become clear. For my part, I'd be pleased to
continue questioning you if you're the same kind of man I am,
otherwise I would drop it. And what kind of man am I? One of
those who would be pleased to be refuted if I say anything
untrue, and who would be pleased to refute anyone who says
anything untrue; one who, however, wouldn't be any less
pleased to be refuted than to refute. For I count being refuted a
greater good, insofar as it is a greater good to be rid of the
greatest evil from oneself than to rid someone else of it. I don't
suppose that any evil for a man is as great as false belief about
the things we're discussing right now. So if you say you're this
b kind of man, too, let's continue the discussion; but if you think
we should drop it, let's be done with it and break it off.

GORGIAS: Oh yes, Socrates, I say that I myself, too, am the sort of person you describe. Still, perhaps we should keep in mind the people who are present here, too. For quite a while ago now, even before you came, I gave them a long presentation, and perhaps we'll stretch things out too long if we continue the discussion. We should think about them, too, so as not to keep any of them who want to do something else. c

CHAEREPHON: You yourselves hear the commotion these men are making, Gorgias and Socrates. They want to hear anything you have to say. And as for myself, I hope I'll never be so busy that I'd forego discussions such as this, conducted in the way this one is, because I find it more practical to do something else.

CALLICLES: By the gods, Chaerephon, as a matter of fact d
I, too, though I've been present at many a discussion before now, don't know if I've ever been so pleased as I am at the moment. So if you're willing to discuss, even if it's all day long, you'll be gratifying me.

SOCRATES: For my part there's nothing stopping me, Callicles, as long as Gorgias is willing.

GORGIAS: It'll be to my shame ever after, Socrates, if I weren't willing, when I myself have made the claim that anyone may ask me anything he wants. All right, if it suits these e
people, carry on with the discussion, and ask what you want.

SOCRATES: Well then, Gorgias, let me tell you what surprises me in the things you've said. It may be that what you said was correct and that I'm not taking your meaning correctly. Do you say that you're able to make an orator out of anyone who wants to study with you?

GORGIAS: Yes.

SOCRATES: So that he'll be persuasive in a gathering about all subjects, not by teaching but by persuading?

GORGIAS: Yes, that's right. 459a

SOCRATES: You were saying just now, mind you, that the orator will be more persuasive even about health than a doctor is.

GORGIAS: Yes I was, more persuasive in a gathering, anyhow.

SOCRATES: And doesn't "in a gathering" just mean "among those who don't have knowledge"? For, among those who do have it, I don't suppose that he'll be more persuasive than the doctor.

GORGIAS: That's true.

SOCRATES: Now if he'll be more persuasive than a doctor, doesn't he prove to be more persuasive than the one who has knowledge?

GORGIAS: Yes, that's right.

b SOCRATES: Even though he's not a doctor, right?

GORGIAS: Yes.

SOCRATES: And a non-doctor, I take it, lacks expertise in the things a doctor's an expert in?

GORGIAS: That's obvious.

SOCRATES: So when an orator is more persuasive than a doctor, a non-knower will be more persuasive than a knower among non-knowers. Isn't this exactly what follows?

GORGIAS: Yes it is, at least in this case.

SOCRATES: The same is true about the orator and oratory relative to the other crafts, too, then. Oratory doesn't need to have any knowledge of the state of their subject matters; it only
c needs to have discovered a persuasion device in order to make itself appear to those who don't have knowledge that it knows more than those who actually do have it.

GORGIAS: Well, Socrates, aren't things made very easy when you come off no worse than the craftsmen even though you haven't learned any other craft but this one?

SOCRATES: Whether the orator does or does not come off worse than the others because of this being so, we'll examine in a moment if it has any bearing on our argument. For now, let's
d consider this point first. Is it the case that the orator is in the same position with respect to what's just and unjust, what's shameful and admirable, what's good and bad, as he is about what's healthy and about the subjects of the other crafts? Does he lack knowledge, that is, of what these are, of what is good or what is bad, of what is admirable or what is shameful, or just or unjust? Does he devise persuasion about them, so that—even though he doesn't know—he seems, among those who don't know either, to know more than someone who actually
e does know? Or is it necessary for him to know, and must the prospective student of oratory already possess this expertise before coming to you? And if he doesn't, will you, the oratory teacher, not teach him any of these things when he comes to

you—for that's not your job—and will you make him seem among most people to have knowledge of such things when in fact he doesn't have it, and to seem good when in fact he isn't? Or won't you be able to teach him oratory at all, unless he knows the truth about these things to begin with? How do matters such as these stand, Gorgias? Yes, by Zeus, do give us 460a
your revelation and tell us what oratory can accomplish, just as you just now said you would.

GORGIAS: Well, Socrates, I suppose that if he really doesn't have this knowledge, he'll learn these things from me as well.

SOCRATES: Hold it there. You're right to say so. If you make someone an orator, it's necessary for him to know what's just and what's unjust, either beforehand, or by learning it from you afterwards.

GORGIAS: Yes, it is.

SOCRATES: Well? A man who has learned carpentry is a b
carpenter, isn't he?

GORGIAS: Yes.

SOCRATES: And isn't a man who has learned music a musician?

GORGIAS: Yes.

SOCRATES: And a man who has learned medicine a doctor? And isn't this so too, by the same reasoning, with the other crafts? Isn't a man who has learned a particular subject the sort of man his expertise makes him?

GORGIAS: Yes, he is.

SOCRATES: And, by this line of reasoning, isn't a man who has learned what's just a just man too?

GORGIAS: Yes, absolutely.

SOCRATES: And a just man does just things, I take it?

GORGIAS: Yes.

SOCRATES: Now isn't an orator necessarily just, and c
doesn't a just man necessarily want to do just things?

GORGIAS: Apparently so.

SOCRATES: Therefore an orator will never want to do what's unjust.

GORGIAS: No, apparently not.

SOCRATES: Do you remember saying a little earlier that
d we shouldn't complain against physical trainers or exile them
from our cities if the boxer uses his boxing skill to do what's
unjust, and that, similarly, if an orator uses his oratorical skill
unjustly we shouldn't complain against his teacher or banish
him from the city, but do so to the one who does what's unjust,
the one who doesn't use his oratorical skill properly? Was that
said or not?

GORGIAS: Yes, it was.

e SOCRATES: But now it appears that this very man, the
orator, would never have done what's unjust, doesn't it?

GORGIAS: Yes, it does.

SOCRATES: And at the beginning of our discussion, Gorgias, it was said that oratory would be concerned with speeches, not those about even and odd, but those about what's just and unjust. Right?

GORGIAS: Yes.

SOCRATES: Well, at the time you said that, I took it that
oratory would never be an unjust thing, since it always makes
its speeches about justice. But when a little later you were
461a saying that the orator could also use oratory unjustly, I was
surprised and thought that your statements weren't consistent,
and so I made that speech in which I said that if you, like me,
think that being refuted is a profitable thing, it would be
worthwhile to continue the discussion, but if you don't, to let it
drop. But now, as we subsequently examine the question, you
see for yourself too that it's agreed that, quite to the contrary,
the orator is incapable of using oratory unjustly and of being
b willing to do what's unjust. By the Dog, Gorgias, it'll take more
than a short session to go through an adequate examination of
how these matters stand!

POLUS: Really, Socrates? Is what you're now saying about
oratory what you actually think of it? Or do you really think,
just because Gorgias was too ashamed not to concede your
further claim that the orator also knows what's just, what's
admirable, and what's good, and that if he came to him without
already having this knowledge to begin with, he said that he
would teach him himself, and then from this admission may-
c be some inconsistency crept into his statements—just the
thing that gives you delight, you're the one who leads him on to

face such questions—who do you think would deny that he himself knows what's just and would teach others? To lead your arguments to such an outcome is a sign of great rudeness.[10]

SOCRATES: Most admirable Polus, it's not for nothing
that we get ourselves companions and sons. It's so that, when
we ourselves have grown older and stumble, you younger men
might be on hand to straighten our lives up again, both in what
we do and what we say. And if Gorgias and I are stumbling
now in what we say—well, you're on hand, straighten us up d
again. That's only right. And if you think we were wrong to
agree on it, I'm certainly willing to retract any of our agreements you like, provided that you're careful about just one
thing.

POLUS: What do you mean?

SOCRATES: That you curb your long style of speech, Polus, the style you tried using at first.

POLUS: Really? Won't I be free to say as much as I like?

SOCRATES: You'd certainly be in a terrible way, my good e
friend, if upon coming to Athens, where there's more freedom
of speech than anywhere else in Greece, you alone should miss
out on it here. But look at it the other way. If you spoke at
length and were unwilling to answer what you're asked,
wouldn't *I* be in a terrible way if I'm not to have the freedom to
stop listening to you and leave? But if you care at all about the 462a
discussion we've had and want to straighten it up, please retract whatever you think best, as I was saying just now. Take
your turn in asking and being asked questions the way Gorgias
and I did, and subject me and yourself to refutation. You say, I
take it, that you're an expert in the same craft as Gorgias is? Or
don't you?

POLUS: Yes, I do.

SOCRATES: And don't you also invite people to ask you each time whatever they like, because you believe you give expert answers?

[10]Polus's indignation at the outcome of Socrates' discussion with Gorgias is evident from the lack of grammatical structure in this speech.

POLUS: Certainly.

b SOCRATES: So now please do whichever of these you like: either ask questions or answer them.

POLUS: Very well, I shall. Tell me, Socrates, since you think Gorgias is confused about oratory, what do *you* say it is?

SOCRATES: Are you asking me what *craft* I say it is?

POLUS: Yes, I am.

SOCRATES: To tell you the truth, Polus, I don't think it's a craft at all.

POLUS: Well then, what do you think oratory is?

SOCRATES: In the treatise that I read recently, it's the

c thing that you say has produced craft.

POLUS: What do you mean?

SOCRATES: I mean a knack.[11]

POLUS: So you think oratory's a knack?

SOCRATES: Yes, I do, unless you say it's something else.

POLUS: A knack for what?

SOCRATES: For producing a certain gratification and pleasure.

POLUS: Don't you think that oratory's an admirable thing, then, to be able to give gratification to people?

SOCRATES: Really, Polus! Have you already discovered

d from me what I say it is, so that you go on to ask me next whether I don't think it's admirable?

POLUS: Haven't I discovered that you say it's a knack?

SOCRATES: Since you value gratification, would you like to gratify me on a small matter?

POLUS: Certainly.

SOCRATES: Ask me now what craft I think pastry baking is.[12]

POLUS: All right, I will. What craft is pastry baking?

[11]Gr. *empeiria*, tr. "experience" at 448c. Socrates uses this word here to deny that oratory meets his conditions of being a *technē*. See n. 4 above.

[12]Gr. *opsopoiia*. The term has a wider use than the translation suggests and can refer to cooking or baking delicacies of various kinds.

SOCRATES: It isn't one at all, Polus. Now say, "What is it then?"

POLUS: All right.

SOCRATES: It's a knack. Say, "A knack for what?"

POLUS: All right.

SOCRATES: For producing gratification and pleasure,
Polus. e

POLUS: So oratory is the same thing as pastry baking?

SOCRATES: Oh no, not at all, although it *is* a part of the same practice.

POLUS: What practice do you mean?

SOCRATES: I'm afraid it may be rather crude to speak the
truth. I hesitate to do so for Gorgias's sake, for fear that he may
think I'm satirizing what he practices. I don't know whether
this is the kind of oratory that Gorgias practices—in fact in our 463a
discussion a while ago we didn't get at all clear on just what he
thinks it is. But what *I* call oratory is a part of some business
that isn't admirable at all.

GORGIAS: Which one's that, Socrates? Say it, and don't spare my feelings.

SOCRATES: Well then, Gorgias, I think there's a practice
that's not craftlike, but one that a mind given to making
hunches takes to, a mind that's bold and naturally clever at
dealing with people. I call it flattery, basically. I think that this b
practice has many other parts as well, and pastry baking, too,
is one of them. This part *seems* to be a craft, but in my account
of it it isn't a craft but a knack and a routine. I call oratory a
part of this, too, along with cosmetics and sophistry. These are
four parts, and they're directed to four objects. So if Polus
wants to discover them, let him do so. He hasn't discovered yet c
what sort of part of flattery I say oratory is. Instead, it's escaped
him that I haven't answered that question yet, and so he goes
on to ask whether I don't consider it to be admirable. And I
won't answer him whether I think it's admirable or shameful
until I first tell what it is. That wouldn't be right, Polus. If,
however, you do want to discover this, ask me what sort of part
of flattery I say oratory is.

POLUS: I shall. Tell me what sort of part it is.

d SOCRATES: Would you understand my answer? By my reasoning, oratory is an image of a part of politics.

POLUS: Well? Are you saying that it's something admirable or shameful?

SOCRATES: I'm saying that it's a shameful thing—I call bad things shameful—since I must answer you as though you already know what I mean.

GORGIAS: By Zeus, Socrates, I myself don't understand what you mean, either!

e SOCRATES: Reasonably enough, Gorgias. I'm not saying anything clear yet. This colt[13] here is youthful and impulsive.

GORGIAS: Never mind him. Please tell me what you mean by saying that oratory is an image of a part of politics.

SOCRATES: All right, I'll try to describe my view of oratory. If this isn't what it actually is, Polus here will refute me.
464a There is, I take it, something you call *body* and something you call *soul*?

GORGIAS: Yes, of course.

SOCRATES: And do you also think that there's a state of fitness for each of these?

GORGIAS: Yes, I do.

SOCRATES: All right. Is there also an apparent state of fitness, one that isn't real? The sort of thing I mean is this. There are many people who *appear* to be physically fit, and unless one is a doctor or one of the fitness experts, one wouldn't readily notice that they're not fit.

GORGIAS: That's true.

SOCRATES: I'm saying that this sort of thing exists in the case of both the body and the soul, a thing that makes the body and the soul *seem* fit when in fact they aren't any the
b more so.

GORGIAS: That's so.

SOCRATES: Come then, and I'll show you more clearly what I'm saying, if I can. I'm saying that of this pair of subjects there are two crafts. The one for the soul I call politics; the one for the body, though it is one, I can't give you a name for offhand, but while the care of the body is a single craft, I'm

[13] A pun on Polus's name: *pōlos* means "colt."

saying it has two parts: gymnastics and medicine. And in politics, the counterpart of gymnastics is legislation, and the part
that corresponds to medicine is justice. Each member of these c
pairs has features in common with the other, medicine with
gymnastics and justice with legislation, because they're concerned with the same thing. They do, however, differ in some
way from each other. These, then, are the four parts, and they
always provide care, in the one case for the body, in the other
for the soul, with a view to what's best. Now flattery takes
notice of them, and—I won't say by *knowing*, but only by
guessing—divides itself into four, masks itself with each of the
parts, and then pretends to be the characters of the masks. It d
takes no thought at all of whatever is best; with the lure of
what's most pleasant at the moment, it sniffs out folly and
hoodwinks it, so that it gives the impression of being most
deserving. Pastry baking has put on the mask of medicine, and
pretends to know the foods that are best for the body, so that if
a pastry baker and a doctor had to compete in front of children, or in front of men just as foolish as children, to determine which of the two, the doctor or the pastry baker, had
expert knowledge of good food and bad, the doctor would die
of starvation. I call this flattery, and I say that such a thing is
shameful, Polus—it's you I'm saying this to—because it guesses 465a
at what's pleasant with no consideration for what's best. And I
say that it isn't a craft, but a knack, because it has no account of
the nature of whatever things it applies by which it applies
them,[14] so that it's unable to state the cause of each thing. And
I refuse to call anything that lacks such an account a craft. If
you have any quarrel with these claims, I'm willing to submit
them for discussion.

So pastry baking, as I say, is the flattery that wears the b
mask of medicine. Cosmetics is the one that wears that of
gymnastics in the same way; a mischievous, deceptive, disgraceful and illiberal thing, one that perpetrates deception by
means of shaping and coloring, smoothing out and dressing

[14]The translation here follows Burnet's text. Dodds's departure from the manuscripts here seems unnecessary and does nothing to improve the intelligibility of the text.

up, so as to make people assume an alien beauty and neglect their own, which comes through gymnastics. So that I won't make a long-style speech, I'm willing to put it to you the way
c the geometers do—for perhaps you follow me now—that what cosmetics is to gymnastics, pastry baking is to medicine; or rather, like this: what cosmetics is to gymnastics, sophistry is to legislation, and what pastry baking is to medicine, oratory is to justice. However, as I was saying, although these activities are naturally distinct in this way, yet because they are so close, sophists and orators tend to be mixed together as people who work in the same area and concern themselves with the same things. They don't know what to do with themselves, and other people don't know what to do with them. In fact, if the soul
d didn't govern the body but the body governed itself, and if pastry baking and medicine weren't kept under observation and distinguished by the soul, but the body itself made judgments about them, making its estimates by reference to the gratification it receives, then the world according to Anaxagoras would prevail, Polus my friend—you're familiar with these views—all things would be mixed together in the same place, and there would be no distinction between matters of medicine and health, and matters of pastry baking.[15]

You've now heard what I say oratory is. It's the counter-
e part in the soul to pastry baking, its counterpart in the body. Perhaps I've done an absurd thing: I wouldn't let you make long speeches, and here I've just composed a lengthy one myself. I deserve to be forgiven, though, for when I made my statements short you didn't understand and didn't know how to deal with the answers I gave you, but you needed a narra-
466a tion. So if I don't know how to deal with your answers either, you must spin out a speech, too. But if I do, just let me deal with them. That's only fair. And if you now know how to deal with my answer, please deal with it.

[15]The opening words of the philosopher Anaxagoras's (500 – 427 B.C.) book, "All things were together," were frequently quoted to describe a state in which all distinctions are obliterated.

POLUS: What is it you're saying, then? You think oratory is flattery?

SOCRATES: I said that it was a *part* of flattery. Don't you remember, Polus, young as you are? What's to become of you?

POLUS: So you think that good orators are held in low regard in their cities, as flatterers?

SOCRATES: Is this a question you're asking, or some b
speech you're beginning?

POLUS: I'm asking a question.

SOCRATES: I don't think they're held in any regard at all.

POLUS: What do you mean, they're not held in any regard? Don't they have the greatest power in their cities?[16]

SOCRATES: No, if by "having power" you mean something that's good for the one who has the power.

POLUS: That's just what I do mean.

SOCRATES: In that case I think that orators have the least power of any in the city.

POLUS: Really? Don't they, like tyrants, put to death anyone they want, and confiscate the property and banish from c
their cities anyone they see fit?

SOCRATES: By the Dog, Polus! I can't make out one way or the other with each thing you're saying whether you're saying these things for yourself and revealing your own view, or whether you're questioning me.

POLUS: I'm questioning you.

SOCRATES: Very well, my friend. In that case, are you asking me two questions at once?

POLUS: What do you mean, two?

SOCRATES: Weren't you just now saying something like "Don't orators, like tyrants, put to death anyone they want, d
don't they confiscate the property of anyone they see fit, and don't they banish them from their cities?"

POLUS: Yes, I was.

[16]Gr. *poleis; polis* (translatable also as "state" or "city-state") refers to a political unit that can encompass many villages spread over the countryside as well as an "urban" center (the *astu*).

SOCRATES: In that case I say that these are two questions, and I'll answer you both of them. I say, Polus, that both orators and tyrants have the least power in their cities, as I was saying
e just now. For they do just about nothing they want to, though they certainly do whatever they see most fit to do.

POLUS: Well, isn't this having great power?

SOCRATES: No; at least Polus says it isn't.

POLUS: I say it isn't? I certainly say it is!

SOCRATES: You certainly don't, by . . . !, since you say that having great power is good for the one who has it.

POLUS: Yes, I do say that.

SOCRATES: Do you think it's good, then, if a person does whatever he sees most fit to do when he lacks intelligence? Do you call this "having great power" too?

POLUS: No, I do not.

SOCRATES: Will you refute me, then, and prove that ora-
467a tors do have intelligence, and that oratory is a craft, and not flattery? If you leave me unrefuted, then the orators who do what they see fit in their cities, and the tyrants, too, won't have gained any good by this. Power is a good thing, you say, but you agree with me that doing what one sees fit without intelligence is bad. Or don't you?

POLUS: Yes, I do.

SOCRATES: How then could it be that orators or tyrants have great power in their cities, so long as Socrates is not refuted by Polus to show that they do what they want?

b POLUS: This fellow—

SOCRATES: —denies that they do what they want. Go ahead and refute me.

POLUS: Didn't you just now agree that they do what they see fit?

SOCRATES: Yes, and I still do.

POLUS: Don't they do what they want, then?

SOCRATES: I say they don't.

POLUS: Even though they do what they see fit?

SOCRATES: That's what I say.

POLUS: What an outrageous thing to say, Socrates! Perfectly monstrous!

SOCRATES: Don't attack me, my peerless Polus, to address you in your own style. Instead, question me if you can, c and prove that I'm wrong. Otherwise you must answer me.

POLUS: All right, I'm willing to answer, to get some idea of what you're saying.

SOCRATES: Do you think that when people do something, they want the thing they're doing at the time, or the thing for the sake of which they do what they're doing? Do you think that people who take medicines prescribed by their doctors, for instance, want what they're doing, the act of taking the medicine, with all its discomfort, or do they want to be healthy, the thing for the sake of which they're taking it?

POLUS: Obviously they want their being healthy.

SOCRATES: With seafarers, too, and those who make d money in other ways, the thing they're doing at the time is not the thing they want—for who wants to make dangerous and troublesome sea voyages? What they want is their being wealthy, the thing for the sake of which, I suppose, they make their voyages. It's for the sake of wealth that they make them.

POLUS: Yes, that's right.

SOCRATES: Isn't it just the same in all cases, in fact? If a person does anything for the sake of something, he doesn't want this thing that he's doing, but the thing for the sake of which he's doing it? e

POLUS: Yes.

SOCRATES: Now is there any thing that isn't either good, or *bad*, or, what is between these, *neither good or bad*?

POLUS: There can't be, Socrates.

SOCRATES: Do you say that wisdom, health, wealth and the like are *good*, and their opposites *bad*?

POLUS: Yes, I do.

SOCRATES: And by things which are *neither* good *nor bad* you mean things which sometimes partake of what's good, sometimes of what's bad, and sometimes of neither, such as 468a sitting or walking, running or making sea voyages, or stones and sticks and the like? Aren't these the ones you mean? Or are there any others that you call *things neither* good *nor bad*?

POLUS: No, these are the ones.

SOCRATES: Now whenever people do things, do they do these intermediate things for the sake of good ones, or the good things for the sake of the intermediate ones?

b POLUS: The intermediate things for the sake of the good ones, surely.

SOCRATES: So it's because we pursue what's good that we walk whenever we walk; we suppose that it's better to walk. And conversely, whenever we stand still, we stand still for the sake of the same thing, what's good. Isn't that so?

POLUS: Yes.

SOCRATES: And don't we also put a person to death, if we do, or banish him and confiscate his property because we suppose that doing that is better for us than not doing it?

POLUS: That's right.

SOCRATES: Hence, it's for the sake of what's good that those who do all these things do them.

POLUS: I agree.

SOCRATES: Now didn't we agree that we want, not those

c things that we do for the sake of something, but that thing for the sake of which we do them?

POLUS: Yes, very much so.

SOCRATES: Hence, we don't simply want to slaughter people, or exile them from their cities and confiscate their property as such; we want to do these things if they are beneficial, but if they're harmful we don't. For we want the things that are good, as you agree, and we don't want those that are neither good nor bad, nor those that are bad. Right? Do you think that what I'm saying is true, Polus, or don't you? Why don't you answer?

POLUS: I think it's true.

d SOCRATES: Since we're in agreement about that then, if a person who's a tyrant or an orator puts somebody to death or exiles him or confiscates his property because he supposes that doing so is better for himself when actually it's worse, this person, I take it, is doing what he sees fit, isn't he?

POLUS: Yes.

SOCRATES: And is he also doing what he wants, if these things are actually bad? Why don't you answer?

POLUS: All right, I don't think he's doing what he wants.

SOCRATES: Can such a man possibly have great power in e
that city, if in fact having great power is, as you agree, something good?

POLUS: He cannot.

SOCRATES: So, what I was saying is true, when I said that it is possible for a man who does in his city what he sees fit not to have great power, nor to be doing what he wants.

POLUS: Really, Socrates! As if *you* wouldn't welcome being in a position to do what you see fit in the city, rather than not! As if *you* wouldn't be envious whenever you'd see anyone putting to death some person he saw fit, or confiscating his property or tying him up!

SOCRATES: Justly, you mean, or unjustly?

POLUS: Whichever way he does it, isn't he to be envied 469a
either way?

SOCRATES: Hush, Polus.

POLUS: What for?

SOCRATES: Because you're not supposed to envy the unenviable or the miserable. You're supposed to pity them.

POLUS: Really? Is this how you think it is with the people I'm talking about?

SOCRATES: Of course.

POLUS: So, you think that a person who puts to death anyone he sees fit, and does so justly, is miserable and to be pitied?

SOCRATES: No, I don't, but I don't think he's to be envied either.

POLUS: Weren't you just now saying that he's miserable?

SOCRATES: Yes, the one who puts someone to death un- b
justly is, my friend, and he's to be pitied besides. But the one who does so justly isn't to be envied.

POLUS: Surely the one who's put to death unjustly is the one who's both to be pitied and miserable.

SOCRATES: Less so than the one putting him to death, Polus, and less than the one who's justly put to death.

POLUS: How can that be, Socrates?

SOCRATES: It's because doing what's unjust is actually the greatest of evils.

POLUS: Really? Is *that* the greatest? Isn't suffering what's unjust a greater one?

SOCRATES: No, not in the least.

POLUS: So you'd want to suffer what's unjust rather than do it?

c SOCRATES: I certainly wouldn't want either, but if it had to be one or the other, I would choose suffering over doing what's unjust.

POLUS: You wouldn't welcome being a tyrant, then?

SOCRATES: No, if by being a tyrant you mean what I do.

POLUS: I mean just what I said a while ago, to be in a position to do whatever you see fit in the city, whether it's putting people to death or exiling them, or doing any and everything just as you see fit.

SOCRATES: Well, my wonderful fellow! I'll put you a
d case, and you criticize it. Imagine me in a crowded marketplace, with a dagger up my sleeve, saying to you, "Polus, I've just got myself some marvelous tyrannical power. So, if I see fit to have any one of these people you see here put to death right on the spot, to death he'll be put. And if I see fit to have one of them have his head bashed in, bashed in it will be, right away. If I see fit to have his coat ripped apart, ripped it will be. That's
e how great my power in this city is!" Suppose you didn't believe me and I showed you the dagger. On seeing it, you'd be likely to say, "But Socrates, *everybody* could have great power that way. For this way any house you see fit might be burned down, and so might the dockyards and triremes of the Athenians, and all their ships, both public and private." But then *that's* not what having great power is, doing what one sees fit. Or do you think it is?

POLUS: No, at least not like that.

470a SOCRATES: Can you then tell me what your reason is for objecting to this sort of power?

POLUS: Yes, I can.

SOCRATES: What is it? Tell me.

POLUS: It's that the person who acts this way is necessarily punished.

SOCRATES: And isn't being punished a bad thing?

POLUS: Yes, it really is.

SOCRATES: Well then, my surprising fellow, here again you take the view that as long as acting as one sees fit coincides with acting beneficially, it is good, and this, evidently, is having great power. Otherwise it is a bad thing, and is having little power. Let's consider this point, too. Do we agree that b
sometimes it's better to do those things we were just now talking about, putting people to death and banishing them and confiscating their property, and at other times it isn't?

POLUS: Yes, we do.

SOCRATES: This point is evidently agreed upon by you and me both?

POLUS: Yes.

SOCRATES: When do you say that it's better to do these things then? Tell me where you draw the line.

POLUS: Why don't you answer that question yourself, Socrates.

SOCRATES: Well then, Polus, if you find it more pleasing c
to listen to me, I say that when one does these things justly, it's better, but when one does them unjustly, it's worse.

POLUS: How hard it is to refute you, Socrates! Why, even a child could refute you and show that what you're saying isn't true!

SOCRATES: In that case, I'll be very grateful to the child, and just as grateful to you if you refute me and rid me of this nonsense. Please don't falter now in doing a friend a good turn. Refute me.

POLUS: Surely, Socrates, we don't need to refer to ancient history to refute you. Why, current events quite suffice to do d
that, and to prove that many people who behave unjustly are happy.

SOCRATES: What sorts of events are these?

POLUS: You can picture this man Archelaus, the son of Perdiccas, ruling Macedonia, I take it?

SOCRATES: Well, if I can't picture him, I do hear things about him.

POLUS: Do you think he's happy or miserable?

SOCRATES: I don't know, Polus. I haven't met the man yet.

e POLUS: Really? You'd know this if you had met him, but without that you don't know straight off that he's happy?

SOCRATES: No, I certainly don't, by Zeus!

POLUS: It's obvious, Socrates, that you won't even claim to know that the Great King is happy![17]

SOCRATES: Yes, and that would be true, for I don't know how he stands in regard to education and justice.

POLUS: Really? Is happiness determined entirely by that?

SOCRATES: Yes, Polus, so I say anyway. I say that the admirable and good person,[18] man or woman, is happy, but that the one who's unjust and wicked is miserable.

471a POLUS: So on your reasoning this man Archelaus is miserable?

SOCRATES: Yes, my friend, if he is in fact unjust.

POLUS: Why of course he's unjust! The sovereignty which he now holds doesn't belong to him at all, given the fact that his mother was a slave of Alcetas, Perdiccas's brother. By rights he was a slave of Alcetas, and if he wanted to do what's just, he'd still be a slave to Alcetas, and on your reasoning would be happy. As it is, how marvelously "miserable"[19] he's turned out to be, now that he's committed the most heinous
b crimes. First he sends for this man, his very own master and uncle, on the pretext of restoring to him the sovereignty that

[17]A title referring to the King of Persia, who embodied the popular idea of supreme happiness.

[18]A literal translation of *kalos k'agathos,* for which no suitable English translation is available. It is used as an epithet to describe the individuals in a society who have attained those goods valued by the society, such as wealth, property, and culture. As views about the proper goods to be valued undergo change, the reference of this term changes correspondingly. In Socrates' usage, the goods in question are moral goods; see 511b, 515e (where his use is sarcastic), 518b, and 527d below.

[19]Scare quotes are used here and elsewhere, where the speaker's use of a term seems clearly sarcastic. The Greek text has no corresponding device.

Perdiccas had taken from him. He entertains him, gets him drunk, both him and his son Alexander, his own cousin and a boy about his own age. He then throws them into a wagon, drives it away at night, and slaughters and disposes of them both. And although he's committed these crimes, he remains unaware of how "miserable" he's become, and feels no remorse either. He refuses to become "happy" by justly bringing up his brother and conferring the sovereignty upon him, the legitimate son of Perdiccas, a boy of about seven to whom the sov- c
ereignty was by rights due to come. Instead, not long afterward, he throws him into a well and drowns him, telling the boy's mother Cleopatra that he fell into the well chasing a goose and lost his life. For this very reason now, because he's committed the most terrible of crimes of any in Macedonia, he's the most "miserable" of all Macedonians instead of the happiest, and no doubt there are some in Athens, beginning with yourself, who'd prefer being any other Macedonian at all to being Archelaus. d

SOCRATES: Already at the start of our discussions, Polus, I praised you because I thought you were well educated in oratory. But I also thought that you had neglected the practice of discussion. And now is *this* all there is to the argument by which even a child could refute me, and do you suppose that when I say that a person who acts unjustly is not happy, I now stand refuted by you by means of *this* argument? Where did you get that idea, my good man? As a matter of fact, I disagree with every single thing you say!

POLUS: You're just unwilling to admit it. You really do e
think it's the way I say it is.

SOCRATES: My wonderful man, you're trying to refute me in oratorical style, the way people in law courts do when they think they're refuting some claim. There, too, one side thinks it's refuting the other when it produces many reputable witnesses on behalf of the arguments it presents, while the person who asserts the opposite produces only one witness, or none at all. This "refutation" is worthless, as far as truth is concerned, for it might happen sometimes that an individual 472a
is brought down by the false testimony of many reputable people. Now too, nearly every Athenian and alien will take your side on the things you're saying, if it's witnesses you want to

produce against me to show that what I say isn't true. Nikias
the son of Niceratus will testify for you, if you like, and his
brothers along with him, the ones whose tripods are standing
in a row in the precinct of Dionysus. Aristocrates the son of
b Scellius will too, if you like, the one to whom that handsome
votive offering in the precinct of Pythian Apollo belongs. And
so will the whole house of Pericles, if you like, or any other
local family you care to choose. Nevertheless, though I'm only
one person, I don't agree with you. You don't compel me; instead you produce many false witnesses against me and try to
banish me from my property, the truth. For my part, if I don't
produce you as a single witness to agree with what I'm saying,
then I suppose I've achieved nothing worth mentioning con-
c cerning the things we've been discussing. And I suppose you
haven't either, if I don't testify on your side, though I'm just one
person, and you disregard all these other people.

There is, then, this style of refutation, the one you and
many others accept. There's also another, one that I accept. Let's
compare the one with the other and see if they'll differ in any
way. It's true, after all, that the matters in dispute between us
are not at all insignificant ones, but pretty nearly those it's
most admirable to have knowledge about, and most shameful
not to. For the heart of the matter is that of recognizing or
d failing to recognize who is happy and who is not. To take first
the immediate question our present discussion's about: you
believe that it's possible for a man who behaves unjustly and
who is unjust to be happy, since you believe Archelaus to be
both unjust and happy. Are we to understand that this is precisely your view?

POLUS: That's right.

SOCRATES: And I say that that's impossible. This is one
point in dispute between us. Fair enough. Although he acts
unjustly, he'll be happy—that is, if he gets his due punishment?

POLUS: Oh no, certainly not! That's how he'd be the most
miserable!

e SOCRATES: But if a man who acts unjustly doesn't get his
due, then, on your reasoning, he'll be happy?

POLUS: That's what I say.

SOCRATES: On my view of it, Polus, a man who acts unjustly, a man who is unjust, is thoroughly miserable, the more so if he doesn't get his due punishment for the wrongdoing he commits, the less so if he pays and receives what is due at the hands of both gods and men.

POLUS: What an absurd position you're trying to main- 473a
tain, Socrates!

SOCRATES: Yes, and I'll try to get you to take the same position too, my good man, for I consider you a friend. For now, these are the points we differ on. Please look at them with me. I said earlier, didn't I, that doing what's unjust is worse than suffering it?

POLUS: Yes, you did.

SOCRATES: And you said that suffering it is worse.

POLUS: Yes.

SOCRATES: And I said that those who do what's unjust are miserable, and was "refuted" by you.

POLUS: You certainly were, by Zeus!

SOCRATES: So you think, Polus. b

POLUS: So I *truly* think.

SOCRATES: Perhaps. And again, you think that those who do what's unjust are happy, so long as they don't pay what is due.

POLUS: I certainly do.

SOCRATES: Whereas I say that they're the most miserable, while those who pay their due are less so. Would you like to refute this too?

POLUS: Why, that's even more "difficult" to refute than the other claim, Socrates!

SOCRATES: Not difficult, surely, Polus. It's impossible. What's true is never refuted.

POLUS: What do you mean? Take a man who's caught
doing something unjust, say, plotting to set himself up as ty- c
rant. Suppose that he's caught, put on the rack, castrated, and has his eyes burned out. Suppose that he's subjected to a host of other abuses of all sorts, and then made to witness his wife and children undergo the same. In the end he's impaled or

tarred. Will he be happier than if he hadn't got caught, had set himself up as tyrant, and lived out his life ruling in his city and doing whatever he liked, a person envied and counted
d happy by fellow citizens and aliens alike? Is *this* what you say is impossible to refute?

SOCRATES: This time you're spooking me, Polus, instead of refuting me. Just before, you were arguing by testimony. Still, refresh my memory on a small point: if the man plots to set himself up as tyrant *unjustly*, you said?

POLUS: Yes, I did.

SOCRATES: In that case neither of them will ever be the happier one, neither the one who gains tyrannical power unjustly, nor the one who pays what is due, for of two miserable people one could not be happier than the other. But the one
e who avoids getting caught and becomes a tyrant is the more miserable one. What's this, Polus? You're laughing? Is this now some further style of refutation, to laugh when somebody makes a point, instead of refuting him?

POLUS: Don't you think you've been refuted already, Socrates, when you're saying things the likes of which no human being would maintain? Just ask any one of these people.

SOCRATES: Polus, I'm not one of the politicians. Last year I was elected to the Council by lot, and when our tribe was presiding and I had to call for a vote, I came in for a
474a laugh.[20] I didn't know how to do it. So please don't tell me to call for a vote from the people present here. If you have no better "refutations" than these to offer, do as I suggested just now: let me have my turn, and you try the kind of refutation I think is called for. For I do know how to produce one witness to whatever I'm saying, and that's the man I'm having a discussion with. The majority I disregard. And I do know how to call for a vote from one man, but I don't even discuss things with

[20]The Council consisted of fifty representatives from each of the ten Athenian tribes. The tribes took turns acting as an executive committee, and a member from the tribe in that position (the *prytanis*) was chosen by lot daily to preside at the meetings of the Council and the Assembly and to put questions to the vote.

the majority. See if you'll be willing to give me a refutation, b
then, by answering the questions you're asked. For I do believe that you and I and everybody else consider doing what's unjust worse than suffering it, and not paying what is due worse than paying it.

POLUS: And I do believe that I don't, and that no other person does, either. So you'd take suffering what's unjust over doing it, would you?

SOCRATES: Yes, and so would you and everyone else.

POLUS: Far from it! I wouldn't, you wouldn't, and nobody else would, either.

SOCRATES: Won't you answer, then? c

POLUS: I certainly will. I'm eager to know what you'll say, in fact.

SOCRATES: So that you'll know, answer me as though this were my first question to you. Which do you think is worse, Polus, doing what's unjust or suffering it?

POLUS: I think suffering it is.

SOCRATES: You do? Which do you think is more shameful, doing what's unjust or suffering it? Tell me.

POLUS: Doing it.

SOCRATES: Now if doing it is in fact more shameful, isn't it also worse?

POLUS: No, not in the least.

SOCRATES: I see. Evidently you don't believe that *admi-* d
rable and *good* are the same, or that *bad* and *shameful* are.[21]

POLUS: No, I certainly don't.

SOCRATES: Well, what about this? When you call all admirable things admirable, bodies, for example, or colors, shapes and sounds, or practices, is it with nothing in view that you do so each time? Take admirable bodies first. Don't you call them

[21]This sentence introduces two pairs of opposites: *kalon* (admirable) and *aischron* (shameful), and *agathon* (good) and *kakon* (bad). Polus denies that the two pairs are co-extensive; Socrates argues that they are. Their meanings, however, are importantly different:

(1) *kalos* (sometimes translatable as "fine," "praiseworthy," "beautiful") is the most general adjective of commendation or approbation in

admirable either in virtue of their usefulness, relative to whatever it is that each is useful for, or else in virtue of some pleasure, if it makes the people who look at them get enjoyment from looking at them? In the case of the admirability of a body, can you mention anything other than these?

e POLUS: No, I can't.

SOCRATES: Doesn't the same hold for all the other things? Don't you call shapes and colors admirable on account of either some pleasure or benefit or both?

POLUS: Yes, I do.

SOCRATES: Doesn't this also hold for sounds and all things musical?

POLUS: Yes.

SOCRATES: And certainly things that pertain to laws and practices—the admirable ones, that is—don't fall outside the limits of being either pleasant or beneficial, or both, I take it.

475a POLUS: No, I don't think they do.

SOCRATES: Doesn't the same hold for the admirability of the fields of learning, too?

POLUS: Yes indeed. Yes, Socrates, your present definition of the admirable in terms of pleasure and good is an admirable one.

SOCRATES: And so is my definition of the shameful in terms of the opposite, pain and evil, isn't it?

POLUS: Necessarily so.

Greek. *Aischros* (translatable also as "base," "disgraceful," "ugly") is correspondingly used to express distaste or disapprobation. They are used in both moral and non-moral contexts.

(2) *agathos* is virtually synonymous with *ophelimos*, "beneficial," and refers to what is beneficial or advantageous, particularly to what is advantageous to an agent. *Kakos* is correspondingly synonymous with *blaberos*, and refers to what is harmful or injurious (to an agent). The sense of these adjectives includes, but is not restricted to, what we would call a moral sense. In the disagreement between Polus and Socrates, for example, about whether doing what is unjust is "worse" than suffering it, it is not the morality of doing versus suffering what is unjust that is in dispute but whether doing it is or is not more harmful (to the agent) than suffering it would be.

SOCRATES: Therefore, whenever one of two admirable things is more admirable than the other, it is so because it surpasses the other either in one of these, pleasure or benefit, or in both.

POLUS: Yes, that's right.

SOCRATES: And whenever one of two shameful things is
more shameful than the other, it will be so because it surpasses b
the other either in pain or in evil. Isn't that necessarily so?

POLUS: Yes.

SOCRATES: Well now, what were we saying a moment ago about doing what's unjust and suffering it? Weren't you saying that suffering it is more evil, but doing it more shameful?

POLUS: I was.

SOCRATES: Now if doing what's unjust is in fact more shameful than suffering it, wouldn't it be so either because it is more painful and surpasses the other in pain, or because it surpasses it in evil, or both? Isn't that necessarily so, too?

POLUS: Of course it is.

SOCRATES: Let's look at this first: does doing what's un- c
just surpass suffering it in pain, and do people who do it hurt more than people who suffer it?

POLUS: No, Socrates, that's not the case at all!

SOCRATES: So it doesn't surpass it in pain, anyhow.

POLUS: Certainly not.

SOCRATES: So, if it doesn't surpass it in pain, it couldn't at this point surpass it in both.

POLUS: Apparently not.

SOCRATES: This leaves it surpassing it only in the other thing.

POLUS: Yes.

SOCRATES: In evil.

POLUS: Evidently.

SOCRATES: So, because it surpasses it in evil, doing what's unjust would be more evil than suffering it.

POLUS: That's clear.

SOCRATES: Now didn't the majority of mankind, and you d
earlier, agree with us that doing what's unjust is more shameful than suffering it?

POLUS: Yes.

SOCRATES: And now, at least, it's turned out to be more evil.

POLUS: Evidently.

SOCRATES: Would you then welcome what's more evil and what's more shameful over what is less so? Don't shrink back from answering, Polus. You won't get hurt in any way. Submit yourself nobly to the argument, as you would to a doctor, and answer me. Say yes or no to what I ask you.

e POLUS: No, I wouldn't, Socrates.

SOCRATES: And would any other person?

POLUS: No, I don't think so, not on this reasoning, anyhow.

SOCRATES: I was right, then, when I said that neither you nor I nor any other person would take doing what's unjust over suffering it, for it really is more evil.

POLUS: So it appears.

SOCRATES: So you see, Polus, that when the one refutation is compared with the other, there is no resemblance at all. Whereas everyone but me agrees with you, you are all I need,
476a although you're just a party of one, for your agreement and testimony. It's you alone whom I call on for a vote; the others I disregard. Let this be our verdict on this matter, then. Let's next consider the second point in dispute between us, that is whether a wrongdoer's paying what is due is the greatest of evils, as you were supposing, or whether his not paying it is a greater one, as I was.

Let's look at it this way. Do you call paying what is due and being justly disciplined for wrongdoing the same?

POLUS: Yes, I do.

b SOCRATES: Can you say, then, that all just things aren't admirable, insofar as they are just? Think carefully and tell me.

POLUS: Yes, I think they are.

SOCRATES: Consider this point, too. If somebody acts upon something, there's necessarily also something that has something done to it by the one acting upon it?

POLUS: Yes, I think so.

SOCRATES: And that it has done to it what the thing acting upon it does, and in the sort of way the thing acting upon it does it? I mean, for example, that if somebody hits, there's necessarily something that is being hit?

POLUS: Necessarily.

SOCRATES: And if the hitter hits hard or quickly, the thing being hit is hit that way, too? c

POLUS: Yes.

SOCRATES: So the thing being hit gets acted upon in whatever way the hitting thing acts upon it?

POLUS: Yes, that's right.

SOCRATES: So, too, if somebody performs surgical burning, then necessarily something is being burned?

POLUS: Of course.

SOCRATES: And if he burns severely or painfully, the thing that's being burned is burned in whatever way the burning thing burns it?

POLUS: That's right.

SOCRATES: Doesn't the same account also hold if a person makes a surgical cut? For something is being cut.

POLUS: Yes.

SOCRATES: And if the cut is large or deep or painful, the thing being cut is cut in whatever way the cutting thing cuts it? d

POLUS: So it appears.

SOCRATES: Summing it up, see if you agree with what I was saying just now, that in all cases, in whatever way the thing acting upon something acts upon it, the thing acted upon is acted upon in just that way.

POLUS: Yes, I do agree.

SOCRATES: Taking this as agreed, is paying what is due a case of being acted upon or of acting upon something?

POLUS: It's necessarily a case of being acted upon, Socrates.

SOCRATES: By someone who acts?

POLUS: Of course. By the one administering discipline.

SOCRATES: Now one who disciplines correctly disciplines justly? e

POLUS: Yes.

SOCRATES: Thereby acting justly, or not?

POLUS: Yes, justly.

SOCRATES: So the one being disciplined is being acted upon justly when he pays what is due?

POLUS: Apparently.

SOCRATES: And it was agreed, I take it, that just things are admirable?

POLUS: That's right.

SOCRATES: So one of these men does admirable things, and the other, the one being disciplined, has admirable things done to him.

POLUS: Yes.

477a SOCRATES: If they're admirable, then, aren't they good? For they're either pleasant or beneficial.

POLUS: Necessarily so.

SOCRATES: Hence, the one paying what is due has good things being done to him?

POLUS: Evidently.

SOCRATES: Hence, he's being benefited?

POLUS: Yes.

SOCRATES: Is his benefit the one I take it to be? Does his soul undergo improvement if he's justly disciplined?

POLUS: Yes, that's likely.

SOCRATES: Hence, one who pays what is due gets rid of evil in his soul?

POLUS: Yes.

SOCRATES: Now, is the evil he gets rid of the most se-
b rious one? Consider it this way: in the matter of a person's financial condition, do you detect any evil other than poverty?

POLUS: No, just poverty.

SOCRATES: What about that of a person's physical condition? Would you say that evil here consists of weakness, disease, ugliness, and the like?

POLUS: Yes, I would.

SOCRATES: Do you believe that there's also some corrupt condition of the soul?

POLUS: Of course.

SOCRATES: And don't you call this condition injustice, ignorance, cowardice, and the like?

POLUS: Yes, certainly.

SOCRATES: Of these three things, one's finances, one's body, and one's soul, you said there are three states of corrup- c tion, namely poverty, disease, and injustice?

POLUS: Yes.

SOCRATES: Which of these states of corruption is the most shameful? Isn't it injustice, and corruption of one's soul in general?

POLUS: Very much so.

SOCRATES: And if it's the most shameful, it's also the most evil?

POLUS: What do you mean, Socrates?

SOCRATES: I mean this: What we agreed on earlier implies that what's most shameful is so always because it's the source either of the greatest pain, or of harm, or of both.

POLUS: Very much so.

SOCRATES: And now we've agreed that injustice, and corruption of soul as a whole, is the most shameful thing. d

POLUS: So we have.

SOCRATES: So either it's most painful and is most shameful because it surpasses the others in pain, or else in harm, or in both?

POLUS: Necessarily so.

SOCRATES: Now is being unjust, undisciplined, cowardly, and ignorant more painful than being poor or sick?

POLUS: No, I don't think so, Socrates, given what we've said, anyhow.

SOCRATES: So the reason that corruption of one's soul is the most shameful of them all is that it surpasses the others by some monstrously great harm and astounding evil, since it e doesn't surpass them in pain, according to your reasoning.

POLUS: So it appears.

SOCRATES: But what is surpassing in greatest harm would, I take it, certainly be the greatest evil there is.

POLUS: Yes.

SOCRATES: Injustice, then, lack of discipline and all other forms of corruption of soul are the greatest evil there is.

POLUS: Apparently so.

SOCRATES: Now, what is the craft that gets rid of poverty? Isn't it that of financial management?

POLUS: Yes.

SOCRATES: What's the one that gets rid of disease? Isn't it that of medicine?

478a POLUS: Necessarily.

SOCRATES: What's the one that gets rid of corruption and injustice? If you're stuck, look at it this way: where and to whom do we take people who are physically sick?

POLUS: To doctors, Socrates.

SOCRATES: Where do we take people who behave unjustly and without discipline?

POLUS: To judges, you mean?

SOCRATES: Isn't it so they'll pay what's due?

POLUS: Yes, I agree.

SOCRATES: Now don't those who administer discipline correctly employ a kind of justice in doing so?

POLUS: That's clear.

SOCRATES: It's financial management, then, that gets rid
b of poverty, medicine that gets rid of disease, and justice that gets rid of injustice and indiscipline.

POLUS: Apparently.

SOCRATES: Which of these, now, is the most admirable?

POLUS: Of which, do you mean?

SOCRATES: Of financial management, medicine, and justice.

POLUS: Justice is by far, Socrates.

SOCRATES: Doesn't it in that case provide either the most pleasure, or benefit, or both, if it really is the most admirable?

POLUS: Yes.

SOCRATES: Now, is getting medical treatment something pleasant? Do people who get it enjoy getting it?

POLUS: No, I don't think so.

SOCRATES: But it *is* beneficial, isn't it?

POLUS: Yes.

SOCRATES: Because they're getting rid of a great evil, so that it's worth their while to endure the pain and so get well. c

POLUS: Of course.

SOCRATES: Now, would a man be happiest, as far as his body goes, if he's under treatment, or if he weren't even sick to begin with?

POLUS: If he weren't even sick, obviously.

SOCRATES: Because happiness evidently isn't a matter of getting rid of evil; it's rather a matter of not even contracting it to begin with.

POLUS: That's so.

SOCRATES: Very well. Of two people, each of whom has an evil in either body or soul, which is the more miserable one, the one who is treated and gets rid of the evil, or the one who doesn't but keeps it? d

POLUS: The one who isn't treated, it seems to me.

SOCRATES: Now, wasn't paying what's due getting rid of the greatest evil, corruption?

POLUS: It was.

SOCRATES: Yes, because such justice makes people self-controlled, I take it, and more just. It proves to be a treatment against corruption.

POLUS: Yes.

SOCRATES: The happiest man, then, is the one who doesn't have evil in his soul, now that this has been shown to be the most serious kind of evil.

POLUS: That's clear.

SOCRATES: And second, I suppose, is the man who gets rid of it. e

POLUS: Evidently.

SOCRATES: This is the man who gets lectured and lashed, the one who pays what is due.

POLUS: Yes.

SOCRATES: The man who keeps it, then, and who doesn't get rid of it, is the one whose life is the worst.

POLUS: Apparently.

SOCRATES: Isn't this actually the man who, although he commits the most serious crimes and uses methods that are

479a most unjust, succeeds in avoiding being lectured and disciplined and paying his due, as Archelaus according to you, and the other tyrants, orators, and potentates have put themselves in a position to do?

POLUS: Evidently.

SOCRATES: Yes, my good man, I take it that these people have managed to accomplish pretty much the same thing as a person who has contracted very serious illnesses, but, by avoiding treatment manages to avoid paying what's due to the doctors for his bodily faults, fearing, as would a child, cauter-
b ization or surgery because they're painful. Don't you think so, too?

POLUS: Yes, I do.

SOCRATES: It's because he evidently doesn't know what health and bodily excellence are like. For on the basis of what we're now agreed on, it looks as though those who avoid paying what is due also do the same sort of thing, Polus. They focus on its painfulness, but are blind to its benefit and are ignorant of how much more miserable it is to live with an unhealthy soul than with an unhealthy body, a soul that's rotten with
c injustice and impiety. This is also the reason they go to any length to avoid paying what is due and getting rid of the greatest evil. They find themselves funds and friends, and ways to speak as persuasively as possible. Now if what we're agreed on is true, Polus, are you aware of what things follow from our argument? Or would you like us to set them out?

POLUS: Yes, if you think we should anyhow.

SOCRATES: Does it follow that injustice, and doing what is unjust, is the greatest evil?

d POLUS: Yes, apparently.

SOCRATES: And it has indeed been shown that paying what is due is what gets rid of this evil?

POLUS: So it seems.

SOCRATES: And that if it isn't paid, the evil is retained?

POLUS: Yes.

SOCRATES: So, doing what's unjust is the second most serious evil. Not paying what's due when one has done what's unjust is by its nature the most serious and foremost evil of all.

POLUS: Evidently.

SOCRATES: Now wasn't this the point in dispute between us, my friend? You considered Archelaus happy, a man who
committed the gravest crimes without paying what was due, e
whereas I took the opposite view, that whoever avoids paying his due for his wrongdoing, whether he's Archelaus or any other man, deserves to be miserable beyond all other men, and that one who does what's unjust is always more miserable than the one who suffers it, and the one who avoids paying what's due always more miserable than the one who does pay it. Weren't these the things I said?

POLUS: Yes.

SOCRATES: Hasn't it been proved that what was said is true?

POLUS: Apparently.

SOCRATES: Fair enough. If these things are true then, 480a
Polus, what is the great use of oratory? For on the basis of what we're agreed on now, what a man should guard himself against most of all is doing what's unjust, knowing that he will have trouble enough if he does. Isn't that so?

POLUS: Yes, that's right.

SOCRATES: And if he or anyone else he cares about acts unjustly, he should voluntarily go to the place where he'll pay his due as soon as possible; he should go to the judge as
though he were going to a doctor, anxious that the disease of b
injustice shouldn't be protracted and cause his soul to fester incurably. What else can we say, Polus, if our previous agreements really stand? Aren't these statements necessarily consistent with our earlier ones in only this way?

POLUS: Well yes, Socrates. What else are we to say?

SOCRATES: So, if oratory is used to defend injustice, Polus, one's own or that of one's relatives, companions, or children, or that of one's country when it acts unjustly, it is of no
use to us at all, unless one takes it to be useful for the opposite c
purpose: that he should accuse himself first and foremost, and then too his family and anyone else dear to him who happens to behave unjustly at any time; and that he should not keep his wrongdoing hidden but bring it out into the open, so that he

may pay his due and get well; and compel himself and the
others not to play the coward, but to grit his teeth and present
himself with grace and courage as to a doctor for cauterization
and surgery, pursuing what's good and admirable without taking any account of the pain. And if his unjust behavior merits
d flogging, he should present himself to be whipped; if it merits
imprisonment, to be imprisoned; if a fine, to pay it; if exile, to
be exiled; and if execution, to be executed. He should be his
own chief accuser, and the accuser of other members of his
family, and use his oratory for the purpose of getting rid of the
greatest evil, injustice, as the unjust acts are being exposed. Are
we to affirm or deny this, Polus?

e POLUS: I think these statements are absurd, Socrates,
though no doubt you think they agree with those expressed
earlier.

SOCRATES: Then either we should abandon those, or else these necessarily follow?

POLUS: Yes, that's how it is.

SOCRATES: And, on the other hand, to reverse the case,
suppose a man had to harm someone, an enemy or anybody at
all, provided that he didn't suffer anything unjust from this
enemy himself—for this is something to be on guard against—
if the enemy did something unjust against another person,
then our man should see to it in every way, both in what he
481a does and what he says, that his enemy does not go to the judge
and pay his due. And if he does go, he should scheme to get
his enemy off without paying what's due. If he's stolen a lot of
gold, he should scheme to get him not to return it but to keep
it and spend it in an unjust and godless way both on himself
and his people. And if his crimes merit the death penalty, he
should scheme to keep him from being executed, preferably
never to die at all but to live forever in corruption, but failing
b that, to have him live as long as possible in that condition. Yes,
this is the sort of thing I think oratory is useful for, Polus, since
for the person who has no intention of behaving unjustly it
doesn't seem to me to have much use—if in fact it has any use
at all—since its usefulness hasn't in any way become apparent
so far.

CALLICLES: Tell me, Chaerephon, is Socrates in earnest about this or is he joking?

CHAEREPHON: I think he's in dead earnest about this, Callicles. There's nothing like asking him, though.

CALLICLES: By the gods! Just the thing I'm eager to do. Tell me, Socrates, are we to take you as being in earnest now, c
or joking? For if you *are* in earnest, and these things you're saying are really true, won't this human life of ours be turned upside down, and won't everything we do evidently be the opposite of what we should do?

SOCRATES: Well, Callicles, if human beings didn't share common experiences, some sharing one, others sharing another, but one of us had some unique experience not shared by others, it wouldn't be easy for him to communicate what he d
experienced to the other. I say this because I realize that you and I are both now actually sharing a common experience: each of the two of us is a lover of two objects, I of Alcibiades, Cleinias' son,[22] and of philosophy, and you of the *demos* [people][23] of Athens, and the Demos who's the son of Pyrilampes. I notice that in each case you're unable to contradict your beloved, clever though you are, no matter what he says or what he claims is so. You keep shifting back and forth. If you say any- e
thing in the Assembly and the Athenian *demos* denies it, you shift your ground and say what it wants to hear. Other things like this happen to you when you're with that good-looking young man, the son of Pyrilampes. You're unable to oppose what your beloveds say or propose, so that if somebody heard you say what you do on their account and was amazed at how absurd that is, you'd probably say—if you were minded to tell him the truth—that unless somebody stops your beloveds from

[22]For an account of Socrates' relationship with Alcibiades, see *Symposium* 215a – 219d. Fascinating and clever, vain and shameless, Alcibiades was the chief instigator of Athens' disastrous expedition against Syracuse in 414 B.C.

[23]The *dēmos* of Athens was its body of citizens. Citizens of Athens decided action and policy by vote in the Assembly, and as jurors in law courts voted to convict or acquit individuals brought to trial.

482a saying what they say, you'll never stop saying these things
either. In that case you must believe that you're bound to hear
me say things like that, too, and instead of being surprised at
my saying them, you must stop my beloved, philosophy, from
saying them. For she always says what you now hear me say,
my dear friend, and she's by far less fickle than my other beloved. As for that son of Cleinias, what he says differs from one
time to the next, but what philosophy says always stays the
b same, and she's saying things that now astound you, although
you were present when they were said. So, either refute her and
show that doing what's unjust without paying what is due for it
is *not* the ultimate of all evils, as I just now was saying it is, or
else, if you leave this unrefuted, then by the Dog, the god of the
Egyptians, Callicles will not agree with you, Callicles, but will be
dissonant with you all your life long. And yet for my part, my
good man, I think it's better to have my lyre or a chorus that I
might lead out of tune and dissonant, and have the vast majority
c of men disagree with me and contradict me, than to be out of
harmony with myself, to contradict myself, though I'm only one
person.

CALLICLES: Socrates, I think you're grandstanding in
these speeches, acting like a true crowd pleaser. Here you are,
playing to the crowd now that Polus has had the same thing
happen to him that he accused Gorgias of letting you do to
him. For he said, didn't he, that when Gorgias was asked by you
d whether he would teach anyone who came to him wanting to
learn oratory but without expertise in what's just, Gorgias was
ashamed and, out of deference to human custom, since people
would take it ill if a person refused, said that he'd teach him.
And because Gorgias agreed on this point, he said, he was
forced to contradict himself, just the thing you like. He
ridiculed you at the time, and rightly so, as I think anyhow.
And now the very same thing has happened to him. And for
this same reason *I* don't approve of Polus: he agreed with you
that doing what's unjust is more shameful than suffering it. As
e a result of this admission he was bound and gagged by you in
the discussion, too ashamed to say what he thought. Although
you claim to be pursuing the truth, you're in fact bringing the

discussion around to the sort of crowd-pleasing vulgarities that are admirable only by law and not by nature.[24] And these, nature and law, are for the most part opposed to each other, so if a person is ashamed and doesn't dare to say what he thinks, 483a
he's forced to contradict himself. This is in fact the clever trick you've thought of, with which you work mischief in your discussions: if a person makes a statement in terms of law, you slyly question him in terms of nature; if he makes it in terms of nature, you question him in terms of law. That's just what happened here, on the question of doing what's unjust versus suffering it. While Polus meant that doing it is more shameful by law, you pursued the argument as though he meant by nature. For by nature all that is more evil is also more shameful, like suffering what's unjust, whereas by law doing it is more shameful. No, no man would put up with suffering what's unjust; b
only a slave would do so, one who is better dead than alive, who when he's treated unjustly and abused can't protect himself or anyone else he cares about. I believe that the people who institute our laws are the weak and the many. They do this, and they assign praise and blame with themselves and their own advantage in mind. They're afraid of the more power- c
ful among men, the ones who are capable of having a greater share, and so they say that getting more than one's share is "shameful" and "unjust," and that doing what's unjust is trying to get more than one's share. They do this so that those people won't get a greater share than they. I think they like getting an equal share, since they are inferior.

These are the reasons why trying to get a greater share than most is said to be unjust and shameful by law and why

[24]Callicles here introduces and later develops the contrast, well known to the fifth century, between *nomos* (law, custom, convention) and *physis* (nature). Along with many (though not all) sophists, Callicles holds that social rules are devised by the weaker members of a society to restrain the stronger. He advocates repudiating such rules and endorses a "law of nature" (483e) according to which the stronger members of a society are entitled to lord it over the weaker and "to have a greater share" than they.

they call it doing what's unjust. But I believe that nature itself
d reveals that it's a just thing for the better man and the more
capable man to have a greater share than the worse man and
the less capable man. Nature shows that this is so in many
places; both among the other animals and in whole cities and
races of men, it shows that this is what justice has been decided to be: that the superior rule the inferior and have a
greater share than they. For what sort of justice did Xerxes go
by when he campaigned against Greece, or his father when he
e campaigned against Scythia?[25] Countless other such examples
could be mentioned. I believe that these men do these things
in accordance with the nature of what's just—yes, by Zeus, in
accordance with the law of nature, and presumably not with
the one we institute. We mold the best and the most powerful
among us, taking them while they're still young, like lion cubs,
and with charms and incantations we subdue them into slav-
484a ery, telling them that one is supposed to get no more than his
fair share, and that that's what's admirable and just. But I believe that if a man whose nature is equal to it were to arise, one
who had shaken off, torn apart, and escaped all this, who had
trampled underfoot our documents, our tricks and charms, and
all our laws that violate nature, he, the slave, would rise up and
be revealed as our master, and here the justice of nature would
b shine forth. I think Pindar, too, refers to what I'm saying in that
song in which he says that

> Law, the king of all
> Of mortals and the immortal gods

—this, he says,

> Brings on and renders just what is most violent
> With towering hand. I take as proof of this
> The deeds of Heracles. For he . . . unbought . . .[26]

[25]The Persian King Xerxes campaigned unsuccessfully against the Greeks in 480/479. The Persian army under the command of his father Darius invaded Scythia in 514 and was all but destroyed at the Danube.

His words are something like that—I don't know the song well—he says that Heracles drove off Geryon's cattle, even though he hadn't paid for them and Geryon hadn't given them to him, on the ground that this is what's just by nature, and c
that cattle and all the other possessions of those who are worse and inferior belong to the one who's better and superior.[27]

This is the truth of the matter, as you will acknowledge if you abandon philosophy and move on to more important things. Philosophy is no doubt a delightful thing, Socrates, as long as one is exposed to it in moderation at the appropriate time of life. But if one spends more time with it than he should, it's the undoing of mankind. For even if one is naturally well favored but engages in philosophy far beyond that appropriate time of life, he can't help but turn out to be inexperienced in everything a man who's to be admirable and good d
and well thought of is supposed to be experienced in. Such people turn out to be inexperienced in the laws of their city or in the kind of speech one must use to deal with people on matters of business, whether in public or private, inexperienced also in human pleasures and appetites and, in short, inexperienced in the ways of human beings altogether. So, when they venture into some private or political activity, they become a laughing stock, as I suppose men in politics do when e
they venture into your pursuits and your kind of speech. What results is Euripides' saying, where he says that "each man shines" in this and "presses on to this,

> allotting the greatest part of the day to this,
> where he finds himself at his best."[28]

---

[26]The poem from which these lines are quoted (or misquoted) has been lost.

[27]The tenth of Heracles' twelve labors for King Eurystheus was to overcome the triple-bodied monster Geryon and take his cattle.

[28]These lines and the other quotations in Callicles' present speech derive from a speech by Zethus, a character in Euripides' lost play, the *Antiope*.

485a And whatever a man's inferior in, he avoids and rails against,
while he praises the other thing, thinking well of himself and
supposing that in this way he's praising himself. I believe,
however, that it's most appropriate to have a share of both. To
partake of as much philosophy as your education requires is
an admirable thing, and it's not shameful to practice philosophy while you're a boy, but when you still do it after you've
grown older and become a man, the thing gets to be ridiculous,
b Socrates! My own reaction to men who philosophize is very
much like that to men who speak haltingly and play like children. When I see a child, for whom it's still quite proper to
make conversation this way, halting in its speech and playing
like a child, I'm delighted. I find it a delightful thing, liberal
and appropriate for the child's age. But when I hear a small
child speaking clearly, I think it's a harsh thing; it hurts my
ears. I think it is something fit for a slave. And when one hears
c a man speaking haltingly or sees him playing like a child, it
strikes me as ridiculous and unmanly, deserving of a flogging.
Now, I react in the same way to men who engage in philosophy, too. When I see philosophy in a young boy, I approve of it;
I think it's appropriate, and consider such a person a liberal
one, whereas I consider one who doesn't engage in philosophy
illiberal, one who'll never count himself deserving of any ad-
d mirable or noble thing. But when I see an older man still
engaging in philosophy and not giving it up, I think such a
man by this time needs a flogging. For, as I was just now saying, it's typical that such a man, even if he's naturally very well
favored, becomes unmanly and avoids the centers of his city
and the marketplaces—in which, according to the poet,[29] men
attain "preeminence"— and, instead, lives the rest of his life in
e hiding, whispering in a corner with three or four boys, never
uttering anything liberal, important, or apt.

Socrates, I do have a rather warm regard for you. I find myself feeling what Zethus, whose words I recalled just now, felt toward Amphion in Euripides' play. In fact, the sorts of things he said to his brother come to my mind to say to you.

[29]Homer, *Iliad* 11. 441.

"You're neglecting the things you should devote yourself to,
Socrates, and though your spirit's nature is so noble, you show
yourself to the world in the shape of a boy. You couldn't put a
speech together correctly before councils of justice or utter any 486a
plausible or persuasive sound. Nor could you make any bold
proposal on behalf of anyone else." And so then, my dear
Socrates—please don't be upset with me, for it's with good will
toward you that I'll say this—don't you think it's shameful to be
the way I take you to be, you and others who ever press on too
far in philosophy? As it is, if someone got hold of you or of
anyone else like you and took you off to prison on the charge
that you're doing something unjust when in fact you aren't, you
can know that you wouldn't have any use for yourself. You'd get
dizzy, your mouth would hang open and you wouldn't know b
what to say. You'd come up for trial and face some no good
wretch of an accuser and be put to death, if death is what he'd
want to condemn you to.[30] And yet, Socrates, "how can this be
a wise thing, the craft which took a well-favored man and
made him worse," able neither to protect himself nor to rescue
himself or anyone else from the gravest dangers, to be robbed
of all of his property by his enemies, and to live a life with c
absolutely no rights in his city? Such a man one could knock
on the jaw without paying what's due for it, to put it rather
crudely. Listen to me, my good man, and stop this refuting.
"Practice the sweet music of an active life and do it where
you'll get a reputation for being intelligent. Leave these sub-
tleties to others"—whether we should call them just silly or
outright nonsense— "which will cause you to live in empty
houses,"[31] and envy not those men who refute such trivia, but
those who have life and renown, and many other good things d
as well.

[30]The dramatic irony in this speech should not be missed. Plato surely expects his readers to recall at this point (as well as at 521b and 522d – e below) the circumstances of Socrates' death.

[31]The bits of this part of Callicles' speech enclosed in quotation marks are recognizably quotations or adaptations taken from the *Antiope*.

SOCRATES: If I actually had a soul made of gold, Callicles, don't you think I'd be pleased to find one of those stones on which they test gold? And if this stone to which I intended to take my soul were the best stone and it agreed that my soul had been well cared for, don't you think I could well know at that point that I'm in good shape and need no further test?

e CALLICLES: What's the point of your question, Socrates?

SOCRATES: I'll tell you. I believe that by running into you, I've run into just such a piece of luck.

CALLICLES: Why do you say that?

SOCRATES: I well know that if you concur with what my
soul believes, then that is the very truth. I realize that the
487a person who intends to put a soul to an adequate test to see
whether it lives rightly or not must have three qualities, all of
which you have: knowledge, good will, and frankness. I run
into many people who aren't able to test me because they're not
wise like you. Others are wise, but they're not willing to tell me
the truth, because they don't care for me the way you do. As for
these two visitors, Gorgias and Polus, they're both wise and
b fond of me, but rather more lacking in frankness, and more
ashamed than they should be. No wonder! They've come to
such a depth of shame that, because they are ashamed, each of
them dares to contradict himself, face to face with many people, and on topics of the greatest importance. You have all
these qualities, which the others don't. You're well-enough educated, as many of the Athenians would attest, and you have
c good will toward me. What's my proof of this? I'll tell you. I
know, Callicles, that there are four of you who've become part-
ners in wisdom, you, Teisander of Aphidnae, Andron the son
of Androtion, and Nausicydes of Cholarges. Once I overheard
you deliberating on how far one should cultivate wisdom, and
I know that some such opinion as this was winning out among
you: you called on each other not to enthusiastically pursue
d philosophizing to the point of pedantry but to be careful not to
become wiser than necessary and so inadvertently bring yourselves to ruin. So, now that I hear you giving me the same advice you gave your closest companions, I have sufficient proof
that you really do have good will toward me. And as to my
claim that you're able to speak frankly without being ashamed,

you yourself say so and the speech you gave a moment ago bears you out. It's clear, then, that this is how these matters stand at the moment. If there's any point in our discussions on e
which you agree with me, then that point will have been adequately put to the test by you and me, and it will not be necessary to put it to any further test, for you'd never have conceded the point through lack of wisdom or excess of shame, and you wouldn't do so by lying to me, either. You are my friend, as you yourself say, too. So, our mutual agreement will really lay hold of truth in the end. Most admirable of all, Callicles, is the examination of those issues about which you took me to task, that of what a man is supposed to be like, and of what he's supposed to devote himself to and how far, when he's 488a
older and when he's young. For my part, if I engage in anything that's improper in my own life, please know well that I do not make this mistake intentionally but out of my ignorance. So don't leave off lecturing me the way you began, but show me clearly what it is I'm to devote myself to, and in what way I might come by it; if you catch me agreeing with you now but at a later time not doing the very things I've agreed upon, then take me for a very stupid fellow and don't bother ever afterward with lecturing me, on the ground that I'm a worthless b
fellow.

Please restate your position for me from the beginning. What is it that you and Pindar hold to be true of what's just by nature? That the superior should take by force what belongs to the inferior, that the better should rule the worse and the more worthy have a greater share than the less worthy? You're not saying anything else, are you? I do remember correctly?

CALLICLES: Yes, that's what I was saying then, and I still say so now, too.

SOCRATES: Is it the same man you call both "better" and "superior"? I wasn't able then, either, to figure out what you c
meant. Is it the stronger ones you call superior, and should those who are weaker take orders from the one who's stronger? That's what I think you were trying to show then also, when you said that large cities attack small ones according to what's just by nature, because they're superior and stronger, assuming that *superior, stronger* and *better* are the same. Or is it possible

for one to be better and also inferior and weaker, or greater but
d more wretched? Or do "better" and "superior" have the same
definition? Please define this for me clearly. Are *superior*, *better* and *stronger* the same or are they different?

CALLICLES: Very well, I'm telling you clearly that they're the same.

SOCRATES: Now aren't the many superior by nature to the one? They're the ones who in fact impose the laws upon the one, as you were saying yourself a moment ago.

CALLICLES: Of course.

SOCRATES: So the rules of the many are the rules of the superior.

CALLICLES: Yes, they are.

e SOCRATES: Aren't they the rules of the better? For by
your reasoning, I take it, the superior are the better.

CALLICLES: Yes.

SOCRATES: And aren't the rules of these people admirable by nature, seeing that they're the superior ones?

CALLICLES: That's my view.

SOCRATES: Now, isn't it a rule of the many that it's just to
have an equal share and that doing what's unjust is more
shameful than suffering it, as you yourself were saying just
489a now? Is this so or not? Be careful that you in your turn don't
get caught being ashamed now. Do the many observe or do they
not observe the rule that it's just to have an equal and not a
greater share, and that doing what's unjust is more shameful
than suffering it? Don't grudge me your answer to this, Callicles, so that if you agree with me I may have my confirmation
from you, seeing that it's the agreement of a man competent to
pass judgment.

CALLICLES: All right, the many do have that rule.

SOCRATES: It's not only by law, then, that doing what's
b unjust is more shameful than suffering it, or just to have an
equal share, but it's so by nature, too. So it looks as though you
weren't saying what's true earlier and weren't right to accuse me
when you said that nature and law were opposed to each other
and that I, well aware of this, am making mischief in my statements, taking any statement someone makes meant in terms of

nature, in terms of law, and any statement meant in terms of law, in terms of nature.

CALLICLES: This man will not stop talking nonsense! Tell me, Socrates, aren't you ashamed, at your age, of trying to catch people's words and of making hay out of someone's trip- c
ping on a phrase? Do you take me to mean by people being *superior* anything else than their being *better*? Haven't I been telling you all along that by "better" and "superior" I mean the same thing? Or do you suppose that I'm saying that if a rubbish heap of slaves and motley men, worthless except perhaps in physical strength, gets together and makes any statements, then these are the rules?

SOCRATES: Fair enough, wisest Callicles. Is this what you're saying?

CALLICLES: It certainly is.

SOCRATES: Well, my marvelous friend, I guessed some d
time ago that it's some such thing you mean by "superior," and I'm questioning you because I'm intent upon knowing clearly what you mean. I don't really suppose that you think two are better than one or that your slaves are better than you just because they're stronger than you. Tell me once more from the beginning, what *do* you mean by *the better*, seeing that it's not *the stronger*? And, my wonderful man, go easier on me in your teaching, so that I won't quit your school.

CALLICLES: You're being ironic, Socrates. e

SOCRATES: No I'm not, Callicles, by Zethus—the character you were invoking in being ironic with me so often just now! But come and tell me: whom do you mean by *the better*?

CALLICLES: I mean the worthier.

SOCRATES: So do you see that you yourself are uttering words, without making anything clear? Won't you say whether by *the better* and *the superior* you mean *the more intelligent*, or some others?

CALLICLES: Yes, by Zeus, they're very much the ones I mean.

SOCRATES: So on your reasoning it will often be the case 490a
that a single intelligent person is superior to countless unintelligent ones, that this person should rule and they be ruled,

and that the one ruling should have a greater share than the ones being ruled. This is the meaning I think you intend—and I'm not trying to catch you with a phrase—if the one is superior to these countless others.

CALLICLES: Yes, that's what I do mean. This is what I take the just by nature to be: that the better one, the more intelligent one, that is, both rules over and has a greater share than his inferiors.

b SOCRATES: Hold it right there! What can your meaning be this time? Suppose we were assembled together in great numbers in the same place, as we are now, and we held in common a great supply of food and drink, and suppose we were a motley group, some strong and some weak, but one of us, being a doctor, was more intelligent about these things. He would, very likely, be stronger than some and weaker than others. Now this man, being more intelligent than we are, will certainly be better and superior in these matters?

CALLICLES: Yes, he will.

c SOCRATES: So should he have a share of this food greater than ours because he's better? Or should he be the one to distribute everything because he's in charge, but not to get a greater share to consume and use up on his own body if he's to escape being punished for it? Shouldn't he, instead, have a greater share than some and a lesser than others, and if he should happen to be the weakest of all, shouldn't the best man have the least share of all, Callicles? Isn't this so, my good man?

CALLICLES: You keep talking of food and drink and doc-
d tors and such nonsense. That's not what I mean!

SOCRATES: Don't you mean that the more intelligent one is the better one? Say yes or no.

CALLICLES: Yes, I do.

SOCRATES: But not that the better should have a greater share?

CALLICLES: Not of food or drink, anyhow.

SOCRATES: I see. Of clothes, perhaps? Should the weaver have the biggest garment and go about wearing the greatest number and the most beautiful clothes?

CALLICLES: What do you mean, clothes?

SOCRATES: But when it comes to shoes, obviously the
most intelligent, the best man in that area should have the e
greater share. Perhaps the cobbler should walk around with the largest and greatest number of shoes on.

CALLICLES: What do you mean, shoes? You keep on with this nonsense!

SOCRATES: Well, if that's not the sort of thing you mean, perhaps it's this. Take a farmer, a man intelligent and admirable and good about land. Perhaps he should have the greater share of seed and use the largest possible quantity of it on his own land.

CALLICLES: How you keep on saying the same things, Socrates!

SOCRATES: Yes, Callicles, not only the same things, but also about the same subjects.

CALLICLES: By the gods! You simply don't let up on your 491a
continual talk of shoemakers and cleaners, cooks and doctors, as if our discussion were about them!

SOCRATES: Won't you say whom it's about, then? What does the superior, the more intelligent man have a greater share of, and have it justly? Will you neither bear with my promptings nor tell me yourself?

CALLICLES: I've been saying it all along. First of all, by the ones who are the superior I don't mean cobblers or cooks,
but those who are intelligent about the affairs of the city, about b
the way it's to be well managed. And not only intelligent, but also brave, competent to accomplish whatever they have in mind, without slackening off because of softness of spirit.

SOCRATES: Do you see, my good Callicles, that you and I are not accusing each other of the same thing? You claim that I'm always saying the same things, and you criticize me for it, whereas I, just the opposite of you, claim that you never say the same things about the same subjects. At one time you were
defining *the better* and *the superior* as *the stronger* then again c
as *the more intelligent*, and now you've come up with something else again: *the superior* and *the better* are now said by

you to be *the braver*. But tell me, my good fellow, once and for all, whom you mean by the better and the superior, and what they're better and superior in.

CALLICLES: But I've already said that I mean those who are intelligent in the affairs of the city, and brave, too. It's fitting
d that they should be the ones who rule their cities, and what's just is that they, as the rulers, should have a greater share than the others, the ruled.

SOCRATES: But what of themselves, my friend?

CALLICLES: What of *what*?

SOCRATES: Ruling or being ruled?

CALLICLES: What do you mean?

SOCRATES: I mean each individual ruling himself. Or is there no need at all for him to rule himself, but only to rule others?

CALLICLES: What do you mean, rule himself?

SOCRATES: Nothing very subtle. Just what the many mean: being self-controlled and master of oneself, ruling the
e pleasures and appetites within oneself.

CALLICLES: How delightful you are! By the self-controlled you mean the stupid ones!

SOCRATES: How so? There's no one who'd fail to recognize that I mean no such thing.

CALLICLES: Yes you do, Socrates, very much so. How could a man prove to be happy if he's enslaved to anyone at all? Rather, this is what's admirable and just by nature—and I'll say it to you now with all frankness—that the man who'll live correctly ought to allow his own appetites to get as large as
492a possible and not restrain them. And when they are as large as possible, he ought to be competent to devote himself to them by virtue of his bravery and intelligence, and to fill them with whatever he may have an appetite for at the time. But this isn't possible for the many, I believe; hence, they become detractors of people like this because of the shame they feel, while they conceal their own impotence. And they say that lack of discipline is shameful, as I was saying earlier, and so they enslave men who are better by nature, and while they themselves lack the ability to provide for themselves fulfillment for their plea-
b sures, their own lack of courage leads them to praise self-con-

trol and justice. As for all those who were either sons of kings
to begin with or else naturally competent to secure some position of rule for themselves as tyrants or potentates, what in
truth could be more shameful and worse than self-control and
justice for these people who, although they are free to enjoy
good things without any interference, should bring as master
upon themselves the law of the many, their talk, and their
criticism? Or how could they exist without becoming miserable under that "admirable" regime of justice and self-control, c
allotting no greater share to their friends than to their enemies,
and in this way "rule" in their cities? Rather, the truth of it,
Socrates—the thing you claim to pursue—is like this: wanton-
ness, lack of discipline, and freedom, if available in good supply, are excellence and happiness; as for these other things,
these fancy phrases, these contracts of men that go against
nature, they're worthless nonsense!

SOCRATES: The way you pursue your argument, speak- d
ing frankly as you do, certainly does you credit, Callicles. For
you are now saying clearly what others are thinking but are
unwilling to say. I beg you, then, not to relax in any way, so that
it may really become clear how we're to live. Tell me: are you
saying that if a person is to be the kind of person he should be,
he shouldn't restrain his appetites but let them become as large
as possible and then should procure their fulfillment from
some source or other, and that this is excellence? e

CALLICLES: Yes, that's what I'm saying.

SOCRATES: So then those who have no need of anything are wrongly said to be happy?

CALLICLES: Yes, for in that case stones and corpses would be happiest.

SOCRATES: But then the life of those people *you* call happiest is a strange one, too. I shouldn't be surprised that Euripides' lines are true when he says:

> But who knows whether being alive is being dead
> And being dead is being alive?[32]

[32]The source of these lines is uncertain.

493a Perhaps in reality we're dead. Once I even heard one of the
wise men say that we are now dead and that our bodies are our
tombs, and that the part of our souls in which our appetites
reside is actually the sort of thing to be open to persuasion and
to shift back and forth. And hence some clever man, a teller of
stories, a Sicilian, perhaps, or an Italian, named this part a jar
[*pithos*], on account of its being a persuadable [*pithanon*] and
suggestible thing, thus slightly changing the name. And fools
b [*anoētoi*] he named *uninitiated* [*amuētoi*], suggesting that that
part of the souls of fools where their appetites are located is
their undisciplined part, one not tightly closed, a leaking jar, as
it were. He based the image on its insatiability. Now this man,
Callicles, quite to the contrary of your view, shows that of the
people in Hades—meaning the unseen [*aides*]—these, the uninitiated ones, would be the most miserable. They would carry
water into the leaking jar using another leaky thing, a sieve.
That's why by the sieve he means the soul (as the man who
c talked with me claimed). And because they leak, he likened
the souls of fools to sieves; for their untrustworthiness and
forgetfulness makes them unable to retain anything. This account is on the whole a bit strange; but now that I've shown it
to you, it does make clear what I want to persuade you to
change your mind about if I can: to choose the orderly life, the
life that is adequate to and satisfied with its circumstances at
any given time instead of the insatiable, undisciplined life. Do
d I persuade you at all, and are you changing your mind to
believe that those who are orderly are happier than those who
are undisciplined, or, even if I tell you many other such stories,
will you change it none the more for that?

CALLICLES: The latter thing you said is the truer, Socrates.

SOCRATES: Come then, and let me give you another image, one from the same school as this one. Consider whether
what you're saying about each life, the life of the self-controlled
man and that of the undisciplined one, is like this: Suppose
there are two men, each of whom has many jars. The jars
e belonging to one of them are sound and full, one with wine,
another with honey, a third with milk, and many others with
lots of other things. And suppose that the sources of each of

these things are scarce and difficult to come by, procurable
only with much toil and trouble. Now the one man, having
filled up his jars, doesn't pour anything more into them and
gives them no further thought. He can relax over them. As for
the other one, he too has resources that can be procured,
though with difficulty, but his containers are leaky and rotten.
He's forced to keep on filling them, day and night, or else he 494a
suffers extreme pain. Now since each life is the way I describe
it, are you saying that the life of the undisciplined man is
happier than that of the orderly man? When I say this, do I at
all persuade you to concede that the orderly life is better than
the undisciplined one, or do I not?

CALLICLES: You do not, Socrates. The man who has
filled himself up has no pleasure any more, and when he's
been filled up and experiences neither joy nor pain, that's living like a stone, as I was saying just now. Rather, living pleas- b
antly consists in this: having as much as possible flow in.

SOCRATES: Isn't it necessary, then, that if there's a lot flowing in, there should also be a lot going out and that there should be big holes for what's passed out?

CALLICLES: Certainly.

SOCRATES: Now you're talking about the life of a stone-curlew[33] instead of that of a corpse or a stone. Tell me, do you say that there is such a thing as hunger, and eating when one is hungry?

CALLICLES: Yes, there is.

SOCRATES: And thirst, and drinking when one is c
thirsty?

CALLICLES: Yes, and also having all other appetites and being able to fill them and enjoy it, and so live happily.

SOCRATES: Very good, my good man! Do carry on the way you've begun, and take care not to be ashamed. And I evidently shouldn't shrink from being ashamed, either. Tell me now first whether a man who has an itch and scratches it and can scratch to his heart's content, scratching his whole life long, can also live happily.

[33]"A bird of messy habits and uncertain identity," Dodds.

d CALLICLES: What nonsense, Socrates. You're a regular crowd pleaser.

SOCRATES: That's just how I shocked Polus and Gorgias and made them be ashamed. *You* certainly won't be shocked, however, or be ashamed, for you're a brave man. Just answer me, please.

CALLICLES: I say that even the man who scratches would have a pleasant life.

SOCRATES: And if a pleasant one, a happy one, too?

CALLICLES: Yes indeed.

e SOCRATES: What if he scratches only his head— or what am I to ask you further? See what you'll answer if somebody asked you one after the other every question that comes next. And isn't the climax of this sort of thing, the life of catamites, a frightfully shameful and miserable one? Or will you have the nerve to say that they are happy as long as they have what they need to their hearts' content?

CALLICLES: Aren't you ashamed, Socrates, to bring our discussion to such matters?

SOCRATES: Is it I who bring them there, my splendid
fellow, or is it the man who claims, just like that, that those
who enjoy themselves, however they may be doing it, are
495a happy, and doesn't discriminate between good kinds of pleasures and bad? Tell me now too whether you say that the
pleasant and the good are the same or whether there is some
pleasure that isn't good.

CALLICLES: Well, to keep my argument from being inconsistent if I say that they're different, I say they're the same.

SOCRATES: You're wrecking your earlier statements, Callicles, and you'd no longer be adequately inquiring into the truth of the matter with me if you speak contrary to what you think.

b CALLICLES: You do it too, Socrates.

SOCRATES: In that case, it isn't right for me to do it, if it's what I do, or for you either. But consider, my marvelous friend, surely the good *isn't* just unrestricted enjoyment. For both those many shameful things hinted at just now obviously follow if this is the case, and many others as well.

CALLICLES: That's your opinion, Socrates.

SOCRATES: Do you really assert these things, Callicles?

CALLICLES: Yes, I do.

SOCRATES: So we're to undertake the discussion on the c
assumption that you're in earnest?

CALLICLES: Most certainly.

SOCRATES: All right, since that's what you think, distinguish the following things for me: There is something you call knowledge, I take it?

CALLICLES: Yes.

SOCRATES: Weren't you also saying just now that there is such a thing as bravery with knowledge?

CALLICLES: Yes, I was.

SOCRATES: Was it just on the assumption that bravery is distinct from knowledge that you were speaking of them as two?

CALLICLES: Yes, very much so.

SOCRATES: Well now, do you say that pleasure and knowledge are the same or different?

CALLICLES: Different of course, you wisest of men. d

SOCRATES: And surely that bravery is different from pleasure, too?

CALLICLES: Of course.

SOCRATES: All right, let's put this on the record: Callicles from Acharnae says that *pleasant* and *good* are the same, and that *knowledge* and *bravery* are different both from each other and from what's *good*.

CALLICLES: And Socrates from Alopece doesn't agree with us about this. Or does he?

SOCRATES: He does not. And I believe that Callicles e
doesn't either when he comes to see himself rightly. Tell me: don't you think that those who do well have the opposite experience of those who do badly?

CALLICLES: Yes, I do.

SOCRATES: Now since these experiences are the opposites of each other, isn't it necessary that it's just the same with them as it is with health and disease? For a man isn't both healthy and sick at the same time, I take it, nor does he get rid of both health and disease at the same time.

CALLICLES: What do you mean?

SOCRATES: Take any part of the body you like, for exam-
496a ple, and think about it. A man can have a disease of the eyes, can't he, to which we give the name "eye disease"?

CALLICLES: Of course.

SOCRATES: But then surely his eyes aren't also healthy at the same time?

CALLICLES: No, not in any way.

SOCRATES: What if he gets rid of his eye disease? Does he then also get rid of his eyes' health and so in the end he's rid of both at the same time?

CALLICLES: No, not in the least.

b SOCRATES: For that, I suppose, is an amazing and unintelligible thing to happen, isn't it?

CALLICLES: Yes, it very much is.

SOCRATES: But he acquires and loses each of them successively, I suppose.

CALLICLES: Yes, I agree.

SOCRATES: Isn't it like this with strength and weakness, too?

CALLICLES: Yes.

SOCRATES: And with speed and slowness?

CALLICLES: Yes, that's right.

SOCRATES: Now, does he acquire and get rid of good things and happiness, and their opposites, bad things and misery, successively too?

CALLICLES: No doubt he does.

c SOCRATES: So if we find things that a man both gets rid of and keeps at the same time, it's clear that these things wouldn't be what's good and what's bad. Are we agreed on that? Think very carefully about it and tell me.

CALLICLES: Yes, I agree most emphatically.

SOCRATES: Go back, now, to what we've agreed on previously. You mentioned hunger—as a pleasant or a painful thing? I mean the hunger itself.

CALLICLES: As a painful thing. But for a hungry man to eat is pleasant.

d SOCRATES: I agree. I understand. But the hunger itself is painful, isn't it?

CALLICLES: So I say.

SOCRATES: And thirst is, too?

CALLICLES: Very much so.

SOCRATES: Am I to ask any further, or do you agree that every deficiency and appetite is painful?

CALLICLES: I do. No need to ask.

SOCRATES: Fair enough. Wouldn't you say that, for a thirsty person, to drink is something pleasant?

CALLICLES: Yes, I would.

SOCRATES: And in the case you speak of, "a thirsty person" means "a person who's in pain," I take it?

CALLICLES: Yes. e

SOCRATES: And drinking is a filling of the deficiency, and is a pleasure?

CALLICLES: Yes.

SOCRATES: Now, don't you mean that insofar as a person is drinking, he's feeling enjoyment?

CALLICLES: Very much so.

SOCRATES: Even though he's thirsty?

CALLICLES: Yes, I agree.

SOCRATES: Even though he's in pain?

CALLICLES: Yes.

SOCRATES: Do you observe the result, that when you say that a thirsty person drinks, you're saying that a person who's in pain simultaneously feels enjoyment? Or doesn't this happen simultaneously in the same place, in the soul or in the body as you like? I don't suppose it makes any difference which. Is this so or not?

CALLICLES: It is.

SOCRATES: But you do say that it's impossible for a person who's doing well to be doing badly at the same time. 497a

CALLICLES: Yes, I do.

SOCRATES: Yet you did agree that it's possible for a person in pain to feel enjoyment.

CALLICLES: Apparently.

SOCRATES: So, feeling enjoyment isn't the same as doing well, and being in pain isn't the same as doing badly, and the result is that what's pleasant turns out to be different from what's good.

CALLICLES: I don't know what your clever remarks amount to, Socrates.

SOCRATES: You do know. You're just pretending you don't, Callicles. Go just a bit further ahead.

CALLICLES: Why do you keep up this nonsense?

b SOCRATES: So you'll know how wise you are in scolding me. Doesn't each of us stop being thirsty and stop feeling pleasure at the same time as a result of drinking?

CALLICLES: I don't know what you mean.

GORGIAS: Don't do that, Callicles! Answer him for our benefit too, so that the discussion may be carried through.

CALLICLES: But Socrates is always like this, Gorgias. He keeps questioning people on matters that are trivial, hardly worthwhile, and refutes them!

GORGIAS: What difference does that make to you? It's none of your business to appraise them, Callicles. You promised Socrates that he could try to refute you in any way he liked.

c CALLICLES: Go ahead, then, and ask these trivial, petty questions, since that's what pleases Gorgias.

SOCRATES: You're a happy man, Callicles, in that you've been initiated into the greater mysteries before the lesser. I didn't think it was permitted. So answer where you left off, and tell me whether each of us stops feeling pleasure at the same time as he stops being thirsty.

CALLICLES: That's my view.

SOCRATES: And doesn't he also stop having pleasures at the same time as he stops being hungry or stops having the other appetites?

CALLICLES: That's so.

SOCRATES: Doesn't he then also stop having pains and
d pleasures at the same time?

CALLICLES: Yes.

SOCRATES: But, he certainly doesn't stop having good things and bad things at the same time, as you agree. Don't you still agree?

CALLICLES: Yes I do. Why?

SOCRATES: Because it turns out that good things are not the same as pleasant ones, and bad things not the same as painful ones. For pleasant and painful things come to a stop simultaneously, whereas good things and bad ones do not, because they are in fact different things. How then could pleasant things be the same as good ones and painful things the same as bad ones?

Look at it this way, too, if you like, for I don't suppose that
you agree with that argument, either. Consider this. Don't you e
call men good because of the presence of good things in them, just as you call them good-looking because of the presence of good looks?

CALLICLES: Yes, I do.

SOCRATES: Well then, do you call foolish and cowardly men good? You didn't a while ago; you were then calling brave and intelligent ones good. Or don't you call these men good?

CALLICLES: Oh yes, I do.

SOCRATES: Well then, have you ever seen a foolish child feel enjoyment?

CALLICLES: Yes, I have.

SOCRATES: But you've never yet seen a foolish man feel enjoyment?

CALLICLES: Yes, I suppose I have. What's the point?

SOCRATES: Nothing. Just answer me. 498a

CALLICLES: Yes, I've seen it.

SOCRATES: Well now, have you ever seen an intelligent man feel pain or enjoyment?

CALLICLES: Yes, I daresay I have.

SOCRATES: Now who feels pain or enjoyment more, intelligent men or foolish ones?

CALLICLES: I don't suppose there's a lot of difference.

SOCRATES: Good enough. Have you ever seen a cowardly man in combat?

CALLICLES: Of course I have.

SOCRATES: Well then, when the enemy retreated, who do you think felt enjoyment more, the cowards or the brave men?

CALLICLES: Both felt it, I think; maybe the cowards felt it b
more. But if not, they felt it to pretty much the same degree.

SOCRATES: It makes no difference. So cowards feel enjoyment too?

CALLICLES: Oh yes, very much so.

SOCRATES: Fools do too, evidently.

CALLICLES: Yes.

SOCRATES: Now when the enemy advances, are the cowards the only ones to feel pain, or do the brave men do so too?

CALLICLES: They both do.

SOCRATES: To the same degree?

CALLICLES: Maybe the cowards feel it more.

SOCRATES: And when the enemy retreats, don't they feel enjoyment more?

CALLICLES: Maybe.

SOCRATES: So don't foolish men and intelligent ones, and cowardly men and brave ones feel enjoyment and pain to
c pretty much the same degree, as you say, or cowardly men feel them more than brave ones?

CALLICLES: That's my view.

SOCRATES: But surely the intelligent and brave men are good and the cowardly and foolish are bad?

CALLICLES: Yes.

SOCRATES: Hence the degree of enjoyment and pain that good and bad men feel is pretty much the same.

CALLICLES: I agree.

SOCRATES: Now are good and bad men pretty much equally both good and bad, or are the bad ones even better?

d CALLICLES: By Zeus! I don't know what you mean.

SOCRATES: Don't you know that you say that the good men are good and the bad men bad because of the presence of good or bad things in them, and that the good things are pleasures and the bad ones pains?

CALLICLES: Yes, I do.

SOCRATES: Aren't good things, pleasures, present in men who feel enjoyment, if in fact they do feel it?

CALLICLES: Of course.

SOCRATES: Now aren't men who feel enjoyment good men, because good things are present in them?

CALLICLES: Yes.

SOCRATES: Well then, aren't bad things, pains, present in men who feel pain?

CALLICLES: They are.

SOCRATES: And you do say that it's because of the presence of bad things that bad men are bad. Or don't you say this any more? e

CALLICLES: Yes, I do.

SOCRATES: So all those who feel enjoyment are good, and all those who feel pain are bad.

CALLICLES: Yes, that's right.

SOCRATES: And those feeling them more are more so, those feeling them less are less so, and those feeling them to pretty much the same degree are good or bad to pretty much the same degree.

CALLICLES: Yes.

SOCRATES: Now aren't you saying that intelligent men and foolish ones, and cowardly and courageous ones, experience pretty much the same degree of enjoyment and pain, or even that cowardly ones experience more of it?

CALLICLES: Yes, I am.

SOCRATES: Join me, then, in adding up what follows for us from our agreements. They say it's an admirable thing to speak of and examine what's admirable "twice and even 499a thrice." We say that the intelligent and brave man is good, don't we?

CALLICLES: Yes.

SOCRATES: And that the foolish and cowardly man is bad?

CALLICLES: Yes, that's right.

SOCRATES: And again, that the man who feels enjoyment is good?

CALLICLES: Yes.

SOCRATES: And the one experiencing pain is bad?

CALLICLES: Necessarily.

SOCRATES: And that the good and the bad man feel pain and enjoyment to the same degree, and that perhaps the bad man feels them even more?

CALLICLES: Yes.

SOCRATES: Doesn't it then turn out that the bad man is both good and bad to the same degree as the good man, or even b that he's better? Isn't this what follows, along with those earlier statements, if one holds that pleasant things are the same as good things? Isn't this necessarily the case, Callicles?

CALLICLES: I've been listening to you for quite some time now, Socrates, and agreeing with you, while thinking that even if a person grants some point to you in jest, you gladly fasten on it, the way boys do. As though you really think that I or anybody else at all don't believe that some pleasures are better and others worse.

SOCRATES: Oh, Callicles! What a rascal you are. You
c treat me like a child. At one time you say that things are one way and at another that the same things are another way, and so you deceive me. And yet I didn't suppose at the beginning that I'd be deceived intentionally by you, because I assumed you were a friend. Now, however, I've been misled, and evidently have no choice but to "make the best with what I have," as the ancient proverb has it, and to accept what I'm given by you. The thing you're saying now, evidently, is that some pleasures are good while others are bad. Is that right?

d CALLICLES: Yes.

SOCRATES: Are the good ones the beneficial ones, and the bad ones the harmful ones?

CALLICLES: Yes, that's right.

SOCRATES: And the beneficial ones are the ones which produce some good, while the bad ones are those that produce some evil?

CALLICLES: That's my view.

SOCRATES: Now, do you mean pleasures like the ones we were just now mentioning in connection with the body, those of eating and drinking? Do some of these produce health in the body, or strength, or some other bodily excellence, and are these pleasures good, while those that produce the opposites
e of these things are bad?

CALLICLES: That's right.

SOCRATES: And similarly, aren't some pains good and others bad, too?

CALLICLES: Of course.

SOCRATES: Now, shouldn't we both choose and act to have the good pleasures and pains?

CALLICLES: Yes, we should.

SOCRATES: But not the bad ones?

CALLICLES: Obviously.

SOCRATES: No, for Polus and I both thought, if you recall, that we should do all things for the sake of what's good, I
take it.[34] Do you also think as we do that the end of all action
is what's good, and that we should do all other things for its
sake, but not it for their sake? Are you voting on our side to 500a
make it three?

CALLICLES: Yes, I am.

SOCRATES: So we should do the other things, including pleasant things, for the sake of good things, and not good things for the sake of pleasant things.

CALLICLES: That's right.

SOCRATES: Now, is it for every man to pick out which kinds of pleasures are good ones and which are bad ones, or does this require a craftsman in each case?

CALLICLES: It requires a craftsman.

SOCRATES: Let's recall what I was actually saying to
Polus and Gorgias.[35] I was saying, if you remember, that there
are some practices that concern themselves with nothing fur- b
ther than pleasure and procure only pleasure, practices that
are ignorant about what's better and worse, while there are
other practices that do know what's good and what's bad. And I
placed the "knack" (not the craft) of pastry baking among
those that are concerned with pleasure, and the medical craft
among those concerned with what's good. And by Zeus, the
god of friendship, Callicles, please don't think that you should
jest with me either, or answer anything that comes to mind,
contrary to what you really think, and please don't accept what
you get from me as though I'm jesting! For you see, don't you, c
that our discussion's about this (and what would even a man of
little intelligence take more seriously than this?), about the

[34] At 467c – 468e.

[35] At 464b – 465a.

way we're supposed to live. Is it the way you urge me toward, to engage in these manly activities, to make speeches among the people, to practice oratory, and to be active in the sort of politics you people engage in these days? Or is it the life spent in philosophy? And in what way does this latter way of life differ
d from the former? Perhaps it's best to distinguish them, as I just tried to do; having done that and having agreed that these are two distinct lives, it's best to examine how they differ from each other, and which of them is the one we should live. Now perhaps you don't yet know what I'm talking about.

CALLICLES: No, I certainly don't.

SOCRATES: Well, I'll tell you more clearly. Given that we're agreed, you and I, that there is such a thing as *good* and such a thing as *pleasant* and that the pleasant is different from the good, and that there's a practice of each of them and a procedure for obtaining it, the quest for the pleasant on the one hand and that for the good on the other—give me first your
e assent to this point or withhold it. Do you assent to it?

CALLICLES: Yes, I do.

SOCRATES: Come then, and agree further with me about what I was saying to them too, if you think that what I said then was true. I was saying, wasn't I, that I didn't think that pastry baking is a craft, but a knack, whereas medicine is a
501a craft. I said that the one, medicine, has investigated both the nature of the object it serves and the cause of the things it does, and is able to give an account of each of these. The other, the one concerned with pleasure, to which the whole of its service is entirely devoted, proceeds toward its object quite inexpertly, without having at all considered either the nature of pleasure or its cause. It does so completely irrationally, with virtually no discrimination. Through routine and knack it merely pre-
b serves the memory of what customarily happens, and that's how it also supplies its pleasures. So, consider first of all whether you think that this account is an adequate one and whether you think that there are also other, similar preoccupations in the case of the soul. Do you think that some of the latter are of the order of crafts and possess forethought about what's best for the soul, while others slight this and have investigated only, as in the other case, the soul's way of getting its

pleasure, without considering which of the pleasures is better or worse, and without having any concern about anything but mere gratification, whether for the better or for the worse? For c
my part, Callicles, I think there are such preoccupations, and I say that this sort of thing is flattery, both in the case of the body and that of the soul and in any other case in which a person may wait upon a pleasure without any consideration of what's better or worse. As for you, do you join us in subscribing to the same opinion on these matters or do you dissent from it?

CALLICLES: No, I won't dissent. I'm going along with you, both to expedite your argument and to gratify Gorgias here.

SOCRATES: Now is this the case with one soul only, and d
not with two or many?

CALLICLES: No, it's also the case with two or many.

SOCRATES: Isn't it also possible to gratify a group of souls collectively at one and the same time, without any consideration for what's best?

CALLICLES: Yes, I suppose so.

SOCRATES: Can you tell me which ones are the practices that do this? Better yet, if you like I'll ask you and you say yes for any which you think falls in this group, and no for any which you think doesn't. Let's look at fluteplaying first. Don't e
you think that it's one of this kind, Callicles? That it merely aims at giving us pleasure without giving thought to anything else?

CALLICLES: Yes, I think so.

SOCRATES: Don't all such practices do that, too? Lyreplaying at competitions, for example?

CALLICLES: Yes.

SOCRATES: What about training choruses and composing dithyrambs? Doesn't that strike you as being something of the same sort? Do you think that Cinesias the son of Meles gives any thought to saying anything of a sort that might lead to the improvement of his audience, or to what is likely to gratify the crowd of spectators?[36] 502a

[36]Cinesias was a dithyrambic poet who was active during the last two decades of the fifth century and the beginning of the fourth. His

CALLICLES: Clearly the latter, Socrates, at least in Cinesias's case.

SOCRATES: What about his father Meles? Do you think he sang to the lyre with a regard for what's best? Or did he fail to regard even what's most pleasant? For he inflicted pain upon his spectators with his singing. But consider whether you don't think that all singing to the lyre and composing of dithyrambs has been invented for the sake of pleasure.

CALLICLES: Yes, I do think so.

b SOCRATES: And what about that majestic, awe-inspiring practice, the composition of tragedy? What is it after? Is the project, the intent of tragic composition merely the gratification of spectators, as you think, or does it also strive valiantly not to say anything that is corrupt, though it may be pleasant and gratifying to them, and to utter in both speech and song anything that might be unpleasant but beneficial, whether the spectators enjoy it or not? In which of these ways do you think tragedy is being composed?

CALLICLES: This much is obvious, Socrates, that it's more
c bent upon giving pleasure and upon gratifying the spectators.

SOCRATES: And weren't we saying just now that this sort of thing is flattery?

CALLICLES: Yes, we were.

SOCRATES: Well then, if one stripped away from the whole composition both melody, rhythm, and meter, does it turn out that what's left is only speeches?

CALLICLES: Necessarily.

SOCRATES: Aren't these speeches given to a large gathering of people?

CALLICLES: I agree.

SOCRATES: So poetry is a kind of popular harangue.[37]

d CALLICLES: Apparently.

---

contemporaries, including Plato, did not for the most part admire the innovations he brought to his art.

[37]Gr. *dēmēgoria*. A cognate noun, *dēmēgoros*, was translated "crowd pleaser" at 482c, where the cognate verb *dēmēgorein* was translated "playing to the crowd."

SOCRATES: And such popular harangue would be oratory, then. Or don't you think that poets practice oratory in the theatres?

CALLICLES: Yes, I do.

SOCRATES : So now we've discovered a popular oratory of a kind that's addressed to men, women, and children, slave and free alike. We don't much like it; we say that it's a flattering sort.

CALLICLES: Yes, that's right.

SOCRATES: Very well. What about the oratory addressed
to the Athenian people and to those in other cities composed e
of free men? What is our view of this kind? Do you think that orators always speak with regard to what's best? Do they always set their sights on making the citizens as good as possible through their speeches? Or are they, too, bent upon the gratification of the citizens and, slighting the common good for the sake of their own private good, do they treat the people like
children, their sole attempt being to gratify them? 503a

CALLICLES: This issue you're asking about isn't just a simple one, for there are those who say what they do because they do care for the citizens, and there are also those like the ones you're talking about.

SOCRATES: That's good enough. For if this matter really has two parts to it, then one part of it would be flattery, I suppose, and shameful public harangue, while the other—that of getting the souls of the citizens to be as good as possible and of striving valiantly to say what is best, whether the audience will find it more pleasant or more unpleasant—is something
admirable. But you've never seen this type of oratory—or, if b
you can mention any orator of this sort, why haven't you let me also know who he is?

CALLICLES: No, by Zeus! I certainly can't mention any of our contemporary orators to you.

SOCRATES: Well then, can you mention anyone from former times through whom the Athenians are reputed to have become better after he began his public addresses, when previously they had been worse? I certainly don't know who this could be.

c CALLICLES: What? Don't they tell you that Themistocles
proved to be a good man, and so did Cimon, Miltiades and
Pericles who died just recently, and whom you've heard speak,
too?[38]

SOCRATES: Yes, Callicles, if the excellence you were
speaking of earlier, the filling up of appetites, both one's own
and those of others, is the true kind. But if this is not, and if
what we were compelled to agree on in our subsequent discussion is the true kind instead—that a man should satisfy those
of his appetites that, when they are filled up, make him better,
d and not those that make him worse, and that this is a matter of
craft—I don't see how I can say that any of these men has
proved to be such a man.

CALLICLES: But if you'll look carefully, you'll find that they were.[39]

SOCRATES: Let's examine the matter calmly and see
whether any of these men has proved to be like that. Well then,
won't the good man, the man who speaks with regard to what's
e best, say whatever he says not randomly but with a view to
something, just like the other craftsmen, each of whom keeps
his own product in view and so does not select and apply
randomly what he applies, but so that he may give his product
some shape? Take a look at painters for instance, if you would,
or housebuilders or shipwrights or any of the other craftsmen
you like, and see how each one places what he does into a
504a certain organization, and compels one thing to be suited for
another and to fit to it until the entire object is put together in

[38]On Themistocles and Pericles see n. 9 above. Miltiades (c. 550 – 489 B.C.) was the leader of the victorious Athenian forces against the Persians at Marathon in 490. Cimon (c. 512 – 449), the son of Miltiades, was an Athenian general and co-founder (with Aristides) of the Delian League. In 468 – 67 he conducted a decisively successful campaign against the Persian fleet.

[39]The translation here follows the manuscript readings. Burnet's text deletes *gegonenai*, which the translation retains. Dodds's text, with its interpolation and transposition of speeches, departs too far from the manuscripts to be reliable here.

an organized and orderly way. The other craftsmen, too, including the ones we were mentioning just lately, the ones concerned with the body, physical trainers and doctors, no doubt give order and organization to the body. Do we agree that this is so or not?

CALLICLES: Let's take it that way.

SOCRATES: So if a house gets to be organized and orderly it would be a good one, and if it gets to be disorganized it would be a terrible one?

CALLICLES: I agree.

SOCRATES: This holds true for a boat, too?

CALLICLES: Yes. b

SOCRATES: And we surely take it to hold true for our bodies, too?

CALLICLES: Yes, we do.

SOCRATES: What about the soul? Will it be a good one if it gets to be disorganized, or if it gets to have a certain organization and order?

CALLICLES: Given what we said before, we must agree that this is so, too.

SOCRATES: Which name do we give to what comes into being in the body as a result or organization and order?

CALLICLES: You mean health and strength, presumably.

SOCRATES: Yes, I do. And which one do we give to what c
comes into being in the soul as a result of organization and order? Try to find and tell me its name, as in the case of the body.

CALLICLES: Why don't you say it yourself, Socrates?

SOCRATES: All right, if that pleases you more, I'll do so. And if you think I'm right, give your assent. If not, refute me and don't give way. I think that the name for the states of organization of the body is "healthy," as a result of which health and the rest of bodily excellence comes into being in it. Is this so or isn't it?

CALLICLES: It is.

SOCRATES: And the name for the states of organization d
and order of the soul is "lawful" and "law," which lead people to become law-abiding and orderly, and these are justice and self-control. Do you assent to this or not?

CALLICLES: Let it be so.

SOCRATES: So this is what that skilled and good orator will look to when he applies to people's souls whatever speeches he makes as well as all of his actions, and any gift he makes or any confiscation he carries out. He will always give
e his attention to how justice may come to exist in the souls of his fellow citizens and injustice be gotten rid of, how self-control may come to exist there and lack of discipline be gotten rid of, and how the rest of excellence may come into being there and evil may depart. Do you agree or not?

CALLICLES: I do.

SOCRATES: Yes, for what benefit is there, Callicles, in giving a body that's sick and in wretched shape lots of very pleasant food or drink or anything else when it won't do the man a bit more good, or, quite to the contrary, when by a fair reckoning it'll do him less good? Is that so?

505a CALLICLES: Let it be so.

SOCRATES: Yes, for I don't suppose that it profits a man to be alive with his body in a terrible condition, for this way his life, too, would be necessarily a wretched one. Or wouldn't it be?

CALLICLES: Yes.

SOCRATES: Now, isn't it also true that doctors generally allow a person to fill up his appetites, to eat when he's hungry, for example, or drink when he's thirsty as much as he wants to when he's in good health, but when he's sick they practically never allow him to fill himself with what he has an appetite for? Do you also go along with this point, at least?

CALLICLES: Yes, I do.

b SOCRATES: And isn't it just the same way with the soul, my excellent friend? As long as it's corrupt, in that it's foolish, undisciplined, unjust and impious, it should be kept away from its appetites and not be permitted to do anything other than what will make it better. Do you agree or not?

CALLICLES: I agree.

SOCRATES: For this is no doubt better for the soul itself?

CALLICLES: Yes, it is.

SOCRATES: Now isn't keeping it away from what it has an appetite for, disciplining it?

CALLICLES: Yes.

SOCRATES: So to be disciplined is better for the soul than lack of discipline, which is what you yourself were thinking just now.

CALLICLES: I don't know what in the world you mean, c
Socrates. Ask somebody else.

SOCRATES: This fellow won't put up with being benefited and with his undergoing the very thing the discussion's about, with being disciplined.

CALLICLES: And I couldn't care less about anything you say, either. I gave you these answers just for Gorgias's sake.

SOCRATES: Very well. What'll we do now? Are we breaking off in the midst of the discussion?

CALLICLES: That's for you to decide.

SOCRATES: They say that it isn't permitted to give up in the middle of telling stories, either. A head must be put on it, d
so that it won't go about headless. Please answer the remaining questions, too, so that our discussion may get its head.

CALLICLES: How unrelenting you are, Socrates! If you'll listen to me, you'll drop this discussion or carry it through with someone else.

SOCRATES: Who else is willing? Surely we mustn't leave the discussion incomplete.

CALLICLES: Couldn't you go through the discussion by yourself, either by speaking in your own person or by answering your own questions?

SOCRATES: In that case Epicharmus's saying applies to e
me: I prove to be sufficient, being "one man, for what two men were saying before."[40] But it looks as though I have no choice at all. Let's by all means do it that way then. I suppose that all of us ought to be contentiously eager to know what's true and what's false about the things we're talking about. That it should become clear is a good common to all. I'll go through the discussion, then, and say how I think it is, and if any of you 506a
thinks that what I agree to with myself isn't so, you must object

[40]Plato considered Epicharmus "the prince of comedy" (*Theaetetus* 152e). The source of the line is not known.

and refute me. For the things I say I certainly don't say with any
knowledge at all; no, I'm searching together with you so that if
my opponent clearly has a point, I'll be the first to concede it.
I'm saying this, however, in case you think the discussion
ought to be carried through to the end. If you don't want it to
be, then let's drop it now and leave.

GORGIAS: No, Socrates, I don't think we should leave yet.
b You must finish the discussion. It seems to me that the others
think so, too. I myself certainly want to hear you go through the
rest of it by yourself.

SOCRATES: All right, Gorgias. I myself would have been
glad to continue my discussion with Callicles here, until I
returned him Amphion's speech for that of Zethus. Well, Callicles, since you're not willing to join me in carrying the discussion through to the end, please do listen to me and interrupt if
c you think I'm saying anything wrong. And if you refute me, I
shan't be upset with you as you were with me; instead you'll go
on record as my greatest benefactor.

CALLICLES: Speak on, my good friend, and finish it up
by yourself.

SOCRATES: Listen, then, as I pick up the discussion from
the beginning. Is the pleasant the same as the good? —It isn't,
as Callicles and I have agreed.— Is the pleasant to be done for
the sake of the good, or the good for the sake of the pleasant? —
The pleasant for the sake of the good.— And *pleasant* is that by
d which, when it's come to be present in us, we feel pleasure, and
good that by which, when it's present in us, we are good? —
That's right.— But surely we are good, both we and everything
else that's good, when some excellence has come to be present
in us? —Yes, I do think that that's necessarily so, Callicles.—
But the best way in which the excellence of each thing comes
to be present in it, whether it's that of an artifact or of a body or
a soul as well, or of any animal, is not just any old way, but is
due to whatever organization, correctness, and craftsmanship
is bestowed on each of them. Is that right? —Yes, I agree.— So
e it's due to organization that the excellence of each thing is
something which is organized and has order? —Yes, I'd say
so.— So it's when a certain order, the proper one for each thing,

comes to be present in it that it makes each of the things there
are, good? — Yes, I think so.— So also a soul which has its own
order is better than a disordered one? —Necessarily so.— But
surely one that has order is an orderly one? —Of course it is.—
And an orderly soul is a self-controlled one? —Absolutely.— 507a
So a self-controlled soul is a good one. I for one can't say
anything else beyond that, Callicles my friend; if you can,
please teach me.

CALLICLES: Say on, my good man.

SOCRATES: I say that if the self-controlled soul is a good
one, then a soul that's been affected the opposite way of the
self-controlled one is a bad one. And this, it's turned out, is the
foolish and undisciplined one. —That's right.— And surely a
self-controlled person would do what's appropriate with respect to both gods and human beings. For if he does what's
inappropriate, he wouldn't be self-controlled. —That's necessarily how it is.— And of course if he did what's appropriate b
with respect to human beings, he would be doing what's just,
and with respect to gods he would be doing what's pious, and
one who does what's just and pious must necessarily be just
and pious. —That's so.— Yes, and he would also necessarily be
brave, for it's not like a self-controlled man to either pursue or
avoid what isn't appropriate, but to avoid and pursue what he
should, whether these are things to do, or people, or pleasures
and pains, and to stand fast and endure them where he should.
So, it's necessarily very much the case, Callicles, that the self- c
controlled man, because he's just and brave and pious, as we've
recounted, is a completely good man, that the good man does
well and admirably whatever he does, and that the man who
does well is blessed and happy, while the corrupt man, the one
who does badly, is miserable. And this would be the one who's
in the condition opposite to that of the self-controlled one, the
undisciplined one whom you were praising.

So this is how I set down the matter, and I say that this is
true. And if it is true, then a person who wants to be happy
must evidently pursue and practice self-control. Each of us d
must flee away from lack of discipline as quickly as his feet
will carry him, and must above all make sure that he has no

need of being disciplined, but if he does have that need, either he himself or anyone in his house, either a private citizen or a whole city, he must pay his due and must be disciplined, if he's to be happy. This is the target to which I think one should look in living, and in his actions he should direct all of his own affairs and those of his city to the end that justice and self-
e control will be present in one who is to be blessed. He should not allow his appetites to be undisciplined or undertake to fill them up—a never ending evil—and live the life of a marauder. Such a man could not be dear to another man or to a god, for he cannot be a partner, and where there's no partnership there's no friendship. Yes, Callicles, wise men claim that partnership
508a and friendship, orderliness, self-control, and justice hold together heaven and earth, and gods and men, and that is why they call this universe a *world order*, my friend, and not an undisciplined world-disorder. I believe that you don't pay attention to these facts, even though you're a wise man in these matters. You've failed to notice that proportionate equality has great power among both gods and men, and you suppose that you ought to practice getting the greater share. That's because you neglect geometry.

Very well. We must either refute this argument and show
b that it's not the possession of justice and self-control that makes happy people happy and the possession of evil that makes miserable people miserable, or else, if this is true, we must consider what the consequences are. These consequences are all those previous things, Callicles, the ones about which you asked me whether I was speaking in earnest when I said that a man should be his own accuser, or his son's or his friend's, if he's done anything unjust, and should use oratory for that purpose. Also what you thought Polus was ashamed to concede is true after all, that doing what's unjust is as much
c more evil than suffering it as it is more shameful, and that a person who is to be an orator the right way should be just and have expert knowledge of what's just, the point Polus in his turn claimed Gorgias to have agreed to out of shame.

That being so, let's examine what it is you're taking me to task for, and whether it's right or not. You say that I'm unable to

protect either myself or any of my friends or relatives or rescue
them from the gravest dangers, and that I'm at the mercy of the
first comer, just as people without rights are, whether he wants
to knock me on the jaw, to use that forceful expression of yours, d
or confiscate my property, or exile me from the city, or ul-
timately put me to death. To be in that position is, by your
reasoning, the most shameful thing of all. As for what my own
reasoning is, that's been told many times by now, but there's
nothing to stop its being told once again. I deny, Callicles, that
being knocked on the jaw unjustly is the most shameful thing,
or that having my body or my purse cut is, and I affirm that to e
knock or cut me or my possessions unjustly is both more
shameful and more evil, and at the same time that to rob or
enslave me or to break into my house or, to sum up, to commit
any unjust act at all against me and my possessions is both
more evil and more shameful for the one who does these unjust acts than it is for me, the one who suffers them. These
conclusions, at which we arrived earlier in our previous discussions are, I'd say, held down and bound by arguments of
iron and adamant, even if it's rather rude to say so. So it would 509a
seem, anyhow. And if you or someone more forceful than you
won't undo them, then anyone who says anything other than
what I'm now saying cannot be speaking well. And yet for my
part, my account is ever the same: I don't know how these
things are, but no one I've ever met, as in this case, can say
anything else without being ridiculous. So once more I set it
down that these things are so. And if they are—if injustice is b
the greatest of evils for the person committing it and if that
person's failure to pay what's due is a greater evil still, if possible, than this one that's the greatest—what is the protection
which would make a man who's unable to provide it for himself truly ridiculous? Isn't it the one that will turn away what
harms us most? Yes, it's necessarily very much the case that
this is the most shameful kind of protection not to be able to
provide, either for oneself or for one's friends or relatives. And
the second kind's the one that turns away the second greatest c
evil, the third kind the one against the third greatest, and so
on. The greater by its nature each evil is, the more admirable it

is to be able to provide protection against it, too, and the more shameful not to be able to. Is this the way it is, Callicles, or is it some other way?

CALLICLES: No, it's not any other way.

SOCRATES: Of these two things, then, of doing what's unjust and suffering it, we say that doing it is the greater evil and suffering it the lesser one. With what, then, might a man
d provide himself to protect himself so that he has both these benefits, the one that comes from not doing what's unjust and the one that comes from not suffering it? Is it power or wish? What I mean is this: Is it when a person doesn't wish to suffer what's unjust that he will avoid suffering it, or when he procures a power to avoid suffering it?

CALLICLES: When he procures a power. That is obvious, at least.

SOCRATES: And what about doing what's unjust? Is it when he doesn't wish to do it, is that sufficient—for he won't
e do it—or should he procure a power and a craft for this, too, so that unless he learns and practices it, he will commit injustice? Why don't you answer at least this question, Callicles? Do you think Polus and I were or were not correct in being compelled to agree in our previous discussion when we agreed that no one does what's unjust because he wants to, but that all who do so do it unwillingly?[41]

510a CALLICLES: Let it be so, Socrates, so you can finish up your argument.

SOCRATES: So we should procure a certain power and craft against this too, evidently, so that we won't do what's unjust.

CALLICLES: That's right.

SOCRATES: What, then, is the craft by which we make sure that we don't suffer anything unjust, or as little as possible? Consider whether you think it's the one I do. This is what I think it is: that one ought either to be a ruler himself in his city or even be a tyrant, or else to be a partisan of the regime in power.

[41]See 480a; 467c – 468e.

CALLICLES: Do you see, Socrates, how ready I am to ap-
plaud you whenever you say anything right? I think that this b
statement of yours is right on the mark.

SOCRATES: Well, consider whether you think that the following statement of mine is a good one, too. I think that the one man who's a friend of another most of all is the one whom the men of old and the wise call a friend, the one who's like the other. Don't you think so, too?

CALLICLES: Yes, I do.

SOCRATES: Now, if in the case of a tyrant who's a savage,
uneducated ruler, there were in his city someone much better
than he, wouldn't the tyrant no doubt be afraid of him and
never be able to be a friend to him with all his heart? c

CALLICLES: That's so.

SOCRATES: Nor would he, the tyrant, be a friend to a man much his inferior, if there were such a man, for the tyrant would despise him and would never take a serious interest in him as a friend.

CALLICLES: That's true, too.

SOCRATES: This leaves only a man of like character, one
who approves and disapproves of the same thing and who is
willing to be ruled by and be subject to the ruler, to be to such
a man a friend worth mentioning. This man will have great
power in that city, and no one will do him any wrong and get d
away with it. Isn't that so?

CALLICLES: Yes.

SOCRATES: So, if some young person in that city were to reflect, "In what way would I be able to have great power and no one treat me unjustly?" this, evidently, would be his way to go: to get himself accustomed from childhood on to like and dislike the same things as the master, and to make sure that he'll be as like him as possible. Isn't that so?

CALLICLES: Yes.

SOCRATES: Now won't this man have achieved immunity
to unjust treatment and great power in his city, as you people e
say?

CALLICLES: Oh, yes.

SOCRATES: And also immunity to unjust action? Or is that far from the case, since he'll be like the ruler who's unjust, and he'll have his great power at the ruler's side? For my part, I think that, quite to the contrary, in this way he'll be making sure he'll have the ability to engage in as much wrongdoing as possible and to avoid paying what's due for doing it. Right?

CALLICLES: Apparently.

511a SOCRATES: So he'll have incurred the greatest evil, when his soul is corrupt and mutilated on account of his imitation of the master and on account of his "power."

CALLICLES: I don't know how you keep twisting our discussion in every direction, Socrates. Or don't you know that this "imitator" will put to death, if he likes, your "non-imitator," and confiscate his property?

b SOCRATES: I do know that, Callicles. I'm not deaf. I hear you say it, and heard Polus just now say it many times, and just about everyone else in the city. But now you listen to me, too. I say that, yes, he'll kill him, if he likes, but it'll be a wicked man killing one who's admirable and good.[42]

CALLICLES: And isn't that just the most irritating thing about it?

SOCRATES: No, not for an intelligent person, anyway, as our discussion points out. Or do you think that a man ought to make sure that his life be as long as possible and that he practice those crafts that ever rescue us from dangers, like the
c oratory that you tell me to practice, the kind that preserves us in the law courts?

CALLICLES: Yes, and by Zeus, that's sound advice for you!

SOCRATES: Well, my excellent fellow, do you think that expertise in swimming is a grand thing?

CALLICLES: No, by Zeus, I don't.

SOCRATES: But it certainly does save people from death whenever they fall into the kind of situation that requires this expertise. But if you think this expertise is a trivial one, I'll
d give you one more important than it, that of helmsmanship, which saves not only souls but also bodies and valuables from the utmost dangers, just as oratory does. This expertise is unassuming and orderly, and does not make itself grand, posturing

[42]See above, n. 18.

as though its accomplishment is so magnificent. But while its
accomplishment is the same as that of the expertise practiced
in the courts, it has earned two obols, I suppose, if it has
brought people safely here from Aegina; and if it has brought
them here from Egypt or the Pontus,[43] then, for that great ser- e
vice, having given safe passage to those I was mentioning just
now, the man himself, his children, valuables, and womenfolk,
and setting them ashore in the harbor, it has earned two drach-
mas, if that much.[44] And the man who possesses the craft and
who has accomplished these feats, disembarks and goes for a
stroll along the seaside and beside his ship, with a modest air.
For he's enough of an expert, I suppose, to conclude that it isn't
clear which ones of his fellow voyagers he has benefited by not
letting them drown in the deep, and which ones he has
harmed, knowing that they were no better in either body or 512a
soul when he set them ashore than they were when they em-
barked. So he concludes that if a man afflicted with serious
incurable physical diseases did not drown, this man is miserable for not dying and has gotten no benefit from him. But if a
man has many incurable diseases in what is more valuable
than his body, his soul, life for that man is not worth living,
and he won't do him any favor if he rescues him from the sea
or from prison or from anywhere else. He knows that for a b
corrupt person it's better not to be alive, for he necessarily lives
badly.

That is why it's not the custom for the helmsman to give
himself glory even though he preserves us, and not the engineer either, who sometimes can preserve us no less well than a
general or anyone else, not to mention a helmsman. For there
are times when he preserves entire cities. You don't think that
he's on a level with the advocate, do you? And yet if he wanted
to say what you people do, Callicles, glorifying his occupation, c
he would smother you with speeches, telling you urgently
that people should become engineers, because nothing else

[43] A region along the southern shore of the Black Sea.

[44] A drachma is six obols. In 409 – 406 B.C. the standard daily wage of a laborer was one drachma.

amounts to anything. And the speech would make his point.
But you nonetheless despise him and his craft, and you'd call
him "engineer" as a term of abuse. You'd be unwilling either to
give your daughter to his son, or take his daughter yourself.
And yet, given your grounds for applauding your own activities, what just reason do you have for despising the engi-
d neer and the others whom I was mentioning just now? I know
that you'd say that you're a better man, one from better stock.
But if "better" does not mean what I take it to mean, and if
instead to preserve yourself and what belongs to you, no matter what sort of person you happen to be, is what excellence is,
then your reproach against engineer, doctor, and all the other
crafts which have been devised to preserve us will prove to be
ridiculous. But, my blessed man, please see whether what's
noble and what's good isn't something other than preserving
e and being preserved. Perhaps one who is truly a man should
stop thinking about how long he will live. He should not be
attached to life but should commit these concerns to the god
and believe the women who say that not one single person can
escape fate. He should thereupon give consideration to how he
might live the part of his life still before him as well as possi-
513a ble. Should it be by becoming like the regime under which he
lives? In that case you should now be making yourself as much
like the Athenian people as possible if you expect to endear
yourself to them and have great power in the city. Please see
whether this profits you and me, my friend, so that what they
say happens to the Thessalian witches when they pull down
the moon won't happen to us.[45] Our choice of this kind of civic
power will cost us what we hold most dear. If you think that
some person or other will hand you a craft of the sort that will
b give you great power in this city while you are unlike the
regime, whether for better or for worse, then in my opinion,
Callicles, you're not well advised. You mustn't be their imitator
but be naturally like them in your own person if you expect to
produce any genuine result toward winning the friendship of

[45]That is, causing an eclipse, the typical feat ascribed to Thessalian witches, as to witches and magicians in general (Dodds).

the Athenian people *[demos]* and, yes, by Zeus, of Demos the son of Pyrilampes to boot. Whoever then turns you out to be most like these men, he'll make you a politician in the way you desire to be one, and an orator, too. For each group of people takes delight in speeches that are given in its own c
character, and resents those given in an alien manner—unless you say something else, my dear friend. Can we say anything in reply to this, Callicles?

CALLICLES: I don't know how it is that I think you're right, Socrates, but the thing that happens to most people has happened to me: I'm not really convinced by you.

SOCRATES: It's your love for the people, Callicles, existing in your soul, that stands against me. But if we closely examine these same matters often and in a better way, you'll be con- d
vinced. Please recall that we said that there are two practices for caring for a particular thing, whether it's the body or the soul.[46] One of them deals with pleasure and the other with what's best and doesn't gratify it but struggles against it. Isn't this how we distinguished them then?

CALLICLES: Yes, that's right.

SOCRATES: Now one of them, the one dealing with pleasure, is ignoble and is actually nothing but flattery, right?

CALLICLES: Let it be so, if you like. e

SOCRATES: Whereas the other one, the one that aims to make the thing we're caring for, whether it's a body or a soul, as good as possible, is the more noble one?

CALLICLES: Yes, that's so.

SOCRATES: Shouldn't we then attempt to care for the city and its citizens with the aim of making the citizens themselves as good as possible? For without this, as we discovered earlier, it does no good to provide any other service if the intentions of 514a
those who are likely to make a great deal of money or take a position of rule over people or some other position of power aren't admirable and good. Are we to put this down as true?

CALLICLES: Certainly, if that pleases you more.

[46] At 500b.

SOCRATES: Suppose, then, Callicles, that you and I were about to take up the public business of the city, and we called on each other to carry out building projects—the major works of construction: walls, or ships, or temples—would we have to
b examine and check ourselves closely, first, to see if we are or are not experts in the building craft, and whom we've learned it from? Would we have to, or wouldn't we?

CALLICLES: Yes, we would.

SOCRATES: And, second, we'd have to check, wouldn't we, whether we've ever built a work of construction in private business, for a friend of ours, say, or for ourselves, and whether this structure is admirable or disgraceful. And if we discovered on examination that our teachers have proved to be good and
c reputable ones, and that the works of construction built by us under their guidance were numerous and admirable, and those built by us on our own after we left our teachers were numerous, too, then, if that were our situation, we'd be wise to proceed to public projects. But if we could point out neither teacher nor construction works, either none at all or else many worthless ones, it would surely be stupid to undertake public projects and to call each other on to them. Shall we say that
d this point is right, or not?

CALLICLES: Yes, we shall.

SOCRATES: Isn't it so in all cases, especially if we attempted to take up public practice and called on each other, thinking we were capable doctors? I'd have examined you, and you me, I suppose: "Well now, by the gods! What is Socrates' own physical state of health? Has there ever been anyone else, slave or free man, whose delivery from illness has been due to Socrates?" And I'd be considering other similar questions about you, I suppose. And if we found no one whose physical
e improvement has been due to us, among either visitors or townspeople, either a man or a woman, then by Zeus, Callicles, wouldn't it be truly ridiculous that people should advance to such a height of folly that, before producing many mediocre as well as many successful results in private practice and before having had sufficient exercise at the craft, they should attempt to "learn pottery on the big jar," as that saying goes, and attempt both to take up public practice themselves and to

call on others like them to do so as well? Don't you think it would be stupid to proceed like that?

CALLICLES: Yes, I do.

SOCRATES: But now, my most excellent fellow, seeing 515a
that you yourself are just now beginning to be engaged in the
business of the city and you call on me and take me to task for
not doing so, shall we not examine each other? "Well now, has
Callicles ever improved any of the citizens? Is there anyone
who was wicked before, unjust, undisciplined, and foolish, a
visitor or townsman, a slave or free man, who because of Callicles has turned out admirable and good?" Tell me, Callicles,
what will you say if somebody asks you these scrutinizing b
questions? Whom will you say you've made a better person
through your association with him? Do you shrink back from
answering—if there even *is* anything you produced while still
in private practice before attempting a public career?

CALLICLES: You love to win, Socrates.

SOCRATES: But it's not for love of winning that I'm asking
you. It's rather because I really do want to know the way, whatever it is, in which you suppose the city's business ought to be
conducted among us. Now that you've advanced to the business c
of the city, are we to conclude that you're devoted to some
objective other than that we, the citizens, should be as good as
possible? Haven't we agreed many times already that this is
what a man active in politics should be doing? Have we or
haven't we? Please answer me. Yes we have. (I'll answer for
you.) So, if this is what a good man should make sure about for
his own city, think back now to those men whom you were
mentioning a little earlier and tell me whether you still think
that Pericles, Cimon, Miltiades, and Themistocles have proved d
to be good citizens.

CALLICLES: Yes, I do.

SOCRATES: So if they were good ones, each of them was obviously making the citizens better than they were before. Was he or wasn't he?

CALLICLES: Yes.

SOCRATES: So when Pericles first began giving speeches among the people, the Athenians were worse than when he gave his last ones?

CALLICLES: Presumably.

SOCRATES: Not "presumably," my good man. It necessarily follows from what we've agreed, if he really was a good citizen.

e CALLICLES: So what?

SOCRATES: Nothing. But tell me this as well. Are the Athenians said to have become better because of Pericles, or, quite to the contrary, are they said to have been corrupted by him? That's what *I* hear, anyhow, that Pericles made the Athenians idle and cowardly, chatterers and money-grubbers, since he was the first to institute wages for them.

CALLICLES: The people you hear say this have cauliflower ears, Socrates.

SOCRATES: Here, though, is something I'm not just hearing. I do know clearly and you do, too, that at first Pericles had a good reputation, and when they were worse, the Athenians never voted to convict him in any shameful deposition. But after he had turned them into "admirable and good" people,
516a near the end of his life, they voted to convict Pericles of embezzlement[47] and came close to condemning him to death, because they thought he was a wicked man, obviously.

CALLICLES: Well? Did that make Pericles a bad man?

SOCRATES: A man like that who cared for donkeys or horses or cattle would at least look bad if he showed these animals kicking, butting, and biting him because of their wildness, when they had been doing none of these things when he
b took them over. Or don't you think that any caretaker of any animal is a bad one who will show his animals to be wilder than when he took them over, when they were gentler? Do you think so or not?

CALLICLES: Oh yes, so I may gratify you.

SOCRATES: In that case gratify me now with your answer, too. Is man one of the animals, too?

CALLICLES: Of course he is.

SOCRATES: Wasn't Pericles a caretaker of men?

[47]The trial took place in the autumn of 430 B.C. Pericles was restored to office in 429 and died later that year.

CALLICLES: Yes.

SOCRATES: Well? Shouldn't he, according to what we agreed just now, have turned them out more just instead of more unjust, if while he cared for them he really was good at c
politics?

CALLICLES: Yes, he should have.

SOCRATES: Now as Homer says, the just are gentle.[48] What do you say? Don't you say the same?

CALLICLES: Yes.

SOCRATES: But Pericles certainly showed them to be wilder than they were when he took them over, and that toward himself, the person he'd least want this to happen to.

CALLICLES: Do you want me to agree with you?

SOCRATES: Yes, if you think that what I say is true.

CALLICLES: So be it, then.

SOCRATES: And if wilder, then both more unjust and worse?

CALLICLES: So be it. d

SOCRATES: So on this reasoning Pericles wasn't good at politics.

CALLICLES: You at least deny that he was.

SOCRATES: By Zeus, you do, too, given what you were agreeing to. Let's go back to Cimon. Tell me: didn't the people he was serving ostracize him so that they wouldn't hear his voice for ten years? And didn't they do the very same thing to Themistocles, punishing him with exile besides? And didn't they vote to throw Miltiades, of Marathon fame, into the pit, and if it hadn't been for the prytanis he would have been e
thrown in?[49] And yet these things would not have happened to

[48]Apparently a reference to the formulaic expression, "wild and not just," which occurs three times in the *Odyssey* (6. 120; 9. 175; 13. 201).

[49]Cimon was ostracized in 461 B.C., but may have been recalled in 457. Themistocles was ostracized, probably in 471. Miltiades was charged with a capital offense and impeached before the Assembly in 489. The *prytanis* was that member of the officiating tribe in the Council chosen daily by lot to preside over the Council and the Assembly (see no. 20 above).

these men if they were good men, as you say they were. At least it's not the case that good drivers are the ones who at the start don't fall out of their chariots but who do fall out after they've cared for their horses and become better drivers themselves. This doesn't happen either in driving or in any other work. Or do you think it does?

CALLICLES: No, I don't.

SOCRATES: So it looks as though our earlier statements
517a were true, that we don't know any man who has proved to be good at politics in this city. You were agreeing that none of our present-day ones has, though you said that some of those of times past had, and you gave preference to these men. But these have been shown to be on equal footing with the men of today. The result is that if these men were orators, they practiced neither the true oratory—for in that case they wouldn't have been thrown out—nor the flattering kind.

CALLICLES: But surely, Socrates, any accomplishment that any of our present-day men produces is a far cry from the sorts of accomplishments produced by any one of the others
b you choose.

SOCRATES: No, my strange friend, I'm not criticizing these men either, insofar as they were servants of the city. I think rather that they proved to be better servants than the men of today, and more capable than they of satisfying the city's appetites. But the truth is that in redirecting its appetites and not giving in to them, using persuasion or constraint to get the citizens to become better, they were really not much dif-
c ferent from our contemporaries. That alone is the task of a good citizen. Yes, I too agree with you that they were more clever than our present leaders at supplying ships and walls and dockyards and many other things of the sort.

Now you and I are doing an odd thing in our conversation. The whole time we've been discussing, we constantly keep drifting back to the same point, neither of us recognizing what the other is saying. For my part, I believe you've agreed many times and recognized that after all this subject of ours
d has two parts, both in the case of the body and the soul. The one part of it is the servient one, enabling us to provide our

bodies with food whenever they're hungry or with drink whenever they're thirsty, and whenever they're cold, with clothes, wraps, shoes, and other things our bodies come to have an appetite for. I'm purposely using the same examples in speaking to you, so that you'll understand the more easily. For these, I think you agree, are the very things a shopkeeper, importer, or
producer can provide, a breadbaker or pastrychef, a weaver or e
cobbler or tanner, so it isn't at all surprising that such a person should think himself and be thought by others to be a caretaker of the body—by everyone who doesn't know that over and above all these practices there's a craft, that of gymnastics and medicine, that really does care for the body and is entitled to rule all these crafts and use their products because of its knowledge of what food or drink is good or bad for bodily
excellence, a knowledge which all of the others lack. That's 518a
why the other crafts are slavish and servient and illiberal, and why gymnastics and medicine are by rights mistresses over them. Now, when I say that these same things hold true of the soul, too, I think you sometimes understand me, and you agree as one who knows what I'm saying. But then a little later you come along saying that there have been persons who've proved
to be admirable and good citizens in the city, and when I b
ask who they are, you seem to me to produce people who in the area of politics are very much the same sort you would produce if I asked you, "Who have proved to be or are good caretakers of bodies?" and you replied in all seriousness, "Thearion the breadbaker, and Mithaecus the author of the book on Sicilian pastry baking, and Sarambus the shopkeeper, because these men have proved to be wonderful caretakers of bodies, the first by providing wonderful loaves of bread,
the second pastry, and the third wine." c

Perhaps you'd be upset if I said to you, "My man, you don't have the slightest understanding of gymnastics. The men you're mentioning to me are servants, satisfiers of appetites! They have no understanding whatever of anything that's admirable and good in these cases. They'll fill and fatten people's bodies, if they get the chance, and besides that, destroy their original flesh as well, all the while receiving their praise!

d The latter, in their turn, thanks to their inexperience, will lay the blame for their illnesses and the destruction of their original flesh not on those who threw the parties, but on any people who happen to be with them at the time giving them advice. Yes, when that earlier stuffing has come bringing sickness in its train much later, then, because it's proved to be unhealthy, they'll blame these people and scold them and do something bad to them if they can, and they'll sing the praises
e of those earlier people, the ones responsible for their ills. Right now you're operating very much like that, too, Callicles. You sing the praises of those who threw parties for these people, and who feasted them lavishly with what they had an appetite for. And they say that *they* have made the city great! But that
519a the city is swollen and festering, thanks to those early leaders, that they don't notice. For they filled the city with harbors and dockyards, walls, and tribute payments and such trash as that, but did so without justice and self-control. So, when that fit of sickness comes on, they'll blame their advisers of the moment and sing the praises of Themistocles and Cimon and Pericles, the ones who are to blame for their ills. Perhaps, if you're not careful, they'll lay their hands on you, and on my friend
b Alcibiades, when they lose not only what they gained but what they had originally as well, even though you aren't responsible for their ills but perhaps accessories to them.

And yet there's a foolish business that I, for one, both see happening now and hear about in connection with our early leaders. For I notice that whenever the city lays its hands on one of its politicians because he does what's unjust, they resent it and complain indignantly that they're suffering terrible things. They've done many good things for the city, and so they're being unjustly brought to ruin by it, so their argument goes.
c But that's completely false. Not a single city leader could ever be brought to ruin by the very city he's the leader of. It looks as though those who profess to be politicians are just like those who profess to be sophists. For sophists, too, even though they're wise in other matters, do this absurd thing: while they claim to be teachers of excellence, they frequently accuse their students of doing them wrong, depriving them of their fees

and withholding other forms of thanks from them, even though
the students have been well served by them. Yet what could be
a more illogical business than this statement, that people d
who've become good and just, whose injustice has been re-
moved by their teacher and who have come to possess justice,
should wrong him—something they can't do? Don't you think
that's absurd, my friend? You've made me deliver a real popular
harangue, Callicles, because you aren't willing to answer.

CALLICLES: And you couldn't speak unless somebody answered you?

SOCRATES: Evidently I could. Anyhow, I *am* stretching e
my speeches out at length now, since you're unwilling to answer me. But, my good man, tell me, by the god of friendship:
don't you think it's illogical that someone who says he's made
someone else good should find fault with that person, charging
that he, whom he himself made to become and to be good, is
after all wicked?

CALLICLES: Yes, I do think so.

SOCRATES: Don't you hear people who say they're educating people for excellence saying things like that?

CALLICLES: Yes, I do. But why would you mention com- 520a
pletely worthless people?

SOCRATES: Why would you talk about those people who,
although they say they're the city's leaders and devoted to making it as good as possible, turn around and accuse it, when the
time comes, of being the most wicked? Do you think they're
any different from those others? Yes, my blessed man, they are
one and the same, the sophist and the orator, or nearly so and
pretty similar, as I was telling Polus. But because you don't see
this, you suppose that one of them, oratory, is something won- b
derful, while you sneer at the other. In actuality, however,
sophistry is more to be admired than oratory, insofar as legislation is more admirable than the administration of justice,
and gymnastics more than medicine. And I, for one, should
have supposed that public speakers and sophists are the only
people not in a position to charge the creature they themselves educate with being wicked to them, or else they simultaneously accuse themselves as well, by this same argument, of

having entirely failed to benefit those whom they say they benefit. Isn't this so?
c CALLICLES: Yes, it is.
SOCRATES: And if what I was saying is true, then they
alone, no doubt, are in a position to offer on terms of honor the
benefit they provide—without charge, as is reasonable. For
somebody who had another benefit conferred on him, one
who, for example, had been turned into a fast runner by a
physical trainer, could perhaps deprive the man of his com-
pensation if the trainer offered him that benefit on his honor,
instead of agreeing on a fixed fee and taking his money as
d closely as possible to the time he imparts the speed. For I don't
suppose that it's by slowness that people act unjustly, but by
injustice. Right?
CALLICLES: Yes.
SOCRATES: So if somebody removes that very thing, injustice, he shouldn't have any fear of being treated unjustly. For
him alone is it safe to offer this benefit on terms of honor, if it's
really true that one can make people good. Isn't that so?
CALLICLES: I agree.
SOCRATES: This, then, is evidently why there's nothing
shameful in taking money for giving advice concerning other
matters such as housebuilding or the other crafts.
e CALLICLES: Yes, evidently.
SOCRATES: But as for this activity, which is concerned
with how a person might be as good as possible and manage
his own house or his city in the best possible way, it's considered shameful to refuse to give advice concerning it unless
somebody pays you money. Right?
CALLICLES: Yes.
SOCRATES: For it's clear that what accounts for this is the
fact that of all the benefits this one alone makes the one who
has had good done to him have the desire to do good in return,
so that we think it's a good sign of someone's having done good
by conferring this benefit that he'll have good done to him in
return, and not a good sign if he won't. Is this how it is?
521a CALLICLES: It is.
SOCRATES: Now, please describe for me precisely the
type of care for the city to which you are calling me. Is it that

of striving valiantly with the Athenians to make them as good as possible, like a doctor, or is it like one ready to serve them and to associate with them for their gratification? Tell me the truth, Callicles. For just as you began by speaking candidly to me, it's only fair that you should continue speaking your mind. Tell me now, too, well and nobly.

CALLICLES: In that case I say it's like one ready to serve.

SOCRATES: So, noblest of men, you're calling on me to be b
ready to flatter.

CALLICLES: Yes, if you find it more pleasant not to mince words, Socrates. Because if you don't do this—

SOCRATES: I hope you won't say what you've said many
times, that anyone who wants to will put me to death. That
way I, too, won't repeat my claim that it would be a wicked
man doing this to a good man. And don't say that he'll confiscate any of my possessions, either, so I won't reply that when
he's done so he won't know how to use them. Rather, just as he
unjustly confiscated them from me, so, having gotten them,
he'll use them unjustly too, and if unjustly, shamefully, and if c
shamefully, badly.

CALLICLES: How sure you seem to me to be, Socrates, that not even one of these things will happen to you! You think that you live out of their way and that you wouldn't be brought to court perhaps by some very corrupt and mean man.

SOCRATES: In that case I really am a fool, Callicles, if I
don't suppose that anything might happen to anybody in this
city. But I know this well: that if I do come into court involved
in one of those perils which you mention, the man who brings d
me in will be a wicked man—for no good man would bring
in a man who is not a wrongdoer—and it wouldn't be at all
strange if I were to be put to death. Would you like me to tell
you my reason for expecting this?

CALLICLES: Yes, I would.

SOCRATES: I believe that I'm one of a few Athenians—so
as not to say I'm the only one, but the only one among our
contemporaries—to take up the true political craft and practice the true politics. This is because the speeches I make on
each occasion do not aim at gratification but at what's best.
They don't aim at what's most pleasant. And because I'm not e

willing to do those clever things you recommend, I won't know what to say in court. And the same account I applied to Polus comes back to me. For I'll be judged the way a doctor would be judged by a jury of children if a pastry chef were to bring accusations against him. Think about what a man like that, taken captive among these people, could say in his defense, if somebody were to accuse him and say, "Children, this man has worked many great evils on you, yes, on you. He destroys the youngest among you by cutting and burning them, and by slim-
522a ming them down and choking them he confuses them. He gives them the most bitter potions to drink and forces hunger and thirst on them. He doesn't feast you on a great variety of sweets the way I do!" What do you think a doctor, caught in such an evil predicament, could say? Or if he should tell them the truth and say, "Yes, children, I was doing all those things in the interest of health," how big an uproar do you think such "judges" would make? Wouldn't it be a loud one?

CALLICLES: Perhaps so.

SOCRATES: I should think so! Don't you think he'd be at a
b total loss as to what he should say?

CALLICLES: Yes, he would be.

SOCRATES: That's the sort of thing I know would happen to me, too, if I came into court. For I won't be able to point out any pleasures that I've provided for them, ones they believe to be services and benefits, while I envy neither those who provide them nor the ones for whom they're provided. Nor will I be able to say what's true if someone charges that I ruin younger people by confusing them or abuse older ones by speaking bitter words against them in public or private. I won't be able to say, that is, "Yes, I say and do all these things in the
c interest of justice, my 'honored judges' "—to use that expression you people use—nor anything else. So presumably I'll get whatever comes my way.

CALLICLES: Do you think, Socrates, that a man in such a position in his city, a man who's unable to protect himself, is to be admired?

SOCRATES: Yes, Callicles, as long as he has that one thing that you've often agreed he should have: as long as he has

protected himself against having spoken or done anything unjust relating to either men or gods. For this is the self-protec- d
tion that you and I often have agreed avails the most. Now if
someone were to refute me and prove that I am unable to
provide *this* protection for myself or for anyone else, I would
feel shame at being refuted, whether this happened in the
presence of many or of a few, or just between the two of us; and
if I were to be put to death for lack of *this* ability, I really would
be upset. But if I came to my end because of a deficiency in
flattering oratory, I know that you'd see me bear my death with
ease. For no one who isn't totally bereft of reason and courage e
is afraid to die; doing what's unjust is what he's afraid of. For of
all evils, the ultimate is that of arriving in Hades with one's
soul stuffed full of unjust actions. If you like, I'm willing to
give you an account showing that this is so.

CALLICLES: All right, since you've gone through the other
things, go through this, too.

SOCRATES: Give ear then—as they put it—to a very fine 523a
account. You'll think that it's a mere tale, I believe, although I
think it's an account, for what I'm about to say I will tell you as
true. As Homer tells it, after Zeus, Poseidon, and Pluto took
over the sovereignty from their father, they divided it among
themselves. Now there was a law concerning human beings
during Cronus's time, one that gods even now continue to observe, that when a man who has lived a just and pious life
comes to his end, he goes to the Isles of the Blessed, to make b
his abode in complete happiness, beyond the reach of evils, but
when one who has lived in an unjust and godless way dies, he
goes to the prison of payment and retribution, the one they call
Tartarus. In Cronus's time, and even more recently during
Zeus's tenure of sovereignty, these men faced living judges
while they were still alive, who judged them on the day they
were going to die. Now the cases were badly decided, so Pluto
and the keepers from the Isles of the Blessed came to Zeus and
told him that people were undeservingly making their way in
both directions. So Zeus said, "All right, I'll put a stop to that. c
The cases are being badly decided at this time because those
being judged are judged fully dressed. They're being judged

while they're still alive. Many," he said, "whose souls are wicked are dressed in handsome bodies, good stock and wealth,
and when the judgment takes place they have many witnesses
appear to testify that they have lived just lives. Now the judges
d are awestruck by these things and pass judgment at a time
when they themselves are fully dressed, too, having put their
eyes and ears and their whole bodies up as screens in front of
their souls. All these things, their own clothing and that of
those being judged, have proved to be obstructive to them.
What we must do first," he said, "is to stop them from knowing
their death ahead of time. Now they do have that knowledge.
This is something that Prometheus has already been told to
e put a stop to. Next, they must be judged when they're stripped
naked of all these things, for they should be judged when
they're dead. The judge, too, should be naked, and dead, and
with only his soul he should study only the soul of each person immediately upon his death, when he's isolated from all
his kinsmen and has left behind on earth all that adornment,
so that the judgment may be a just one. Now I, realizing this
before you did, have already appointed my sons as judges, two
from Asia, Minos and Rhadamanthus, and one from Europe,
524a Aiacus. After they've died, they'll serve as judges in the mead-
ow, at the three-way crossing from which the two roads go on,
the one to the Isles of the Blessed and the other to Tartarus.
Rhadamanthus will judge the people from Asia and Aiacus
those from Europe. I'll give seniority to Minos to render final
judgment if the other two are at all perplexed, so that the
judgment concerning the passage of humankind may be as just
as possible."

This, Callicles, is what I've heard, and I believe that it's
b true. And on the basis of these accounts I conclude that something like this takes place: Death, I think, is actually nothing
but the separation of two things from each other, the soul and
the body. So, after they're separated, each of them stays in a
condition not much worse than what it was in when the person was alive. The body retains its nature, and the care it had
received as well as the things that have happened to it are all
c evident. If a man had a body, for instance, which was large

(either by nature or through nurture, or both) while he was alive, his corpse after he has died is large, too. And if it was fat, so is the corpse of the dead man, and so on. And if a man took care to grow his hair long, his corpse will have long hair, too. And again, if a man had been a criminal whipped for his crime and showed scars, traces of beatings on his body inflicted by whips or other blows while he was alive, his body can be seen to have these marks, too, when he is dead. And if a man's limbs were broken or twisted while he was alive, these very things
will be evident, too, when he is dead. In a word, however a d
man treated his body while he was alive, all the marks of that treatment, or most of them, are evident for some time even after he is dead. And I think that the same thing, therefore, holds true also for the soul, Callicles. All that's in the soul is evident after it has been stripped naked of the body, both things that are natural to it and things that have happened to it, things that the person came to have in his soul as a result of his pursuit of each objective. So when they arrive before their
judge—the people from Asia before Rhadamanthus—Rhada- e
manthus brings them to a halt and studies each person's soul without knowing whose it is. He's often gotten hold of the Great King, or some other king or potentate, and noticed that
there's nothing sound in his soul but that it's been thoroughly 525a
whipped and covered with scars, the results of acts of perjury and of injustice, things that each of his actions has stamped upon his soul. Everything was warped as a result of deception and pretense, and nothing was straight, all because the soul had been nurtured without truth. And he saw that the soul was full of distortion and ugliness due to license and luxury, arrogance and incontinence in its actions. And when he had seen it, he dismissed this soul in dishonor straight to the guardhouse, where it went to await suffering its appropriate fate.

It is appropriate for everyone who is subject to punish- b
ment rightly inflicted by another either to become better and profit from it, or else to be made an example for others, so that when they see him suffering whatever it is he suffers, they may be afraid and become better. Those who are benefited, who are

made to pay their due by gods and men, are the ones whose
errors are curable; even so, their benefit comes to them, both
here and in Hades, by way of pain and suffering, for there is no
other possible way to get rid of injustice. From among those
c who have committed the ultimate wrongs and who because of
such crimes have become incurable come the ones who are
made examples of. These persons themselves no longer derive
any profit from their punishment, because they're incurable.
Others, however, do profit from it when they see them undergoing for all time the most grievous, intensely painful and
frightening sufferings for their errors, simply strung up there in
the prison in Hades as examples, visible warnings to unjust
d men who are ever arriving. I claim that Archelaus, too, will be
one of their number, if what Polus says is true, and anyone else
who's a tyrant like him. I suppose that in fact the majority of
these examples have come from the ranks of tyrants, kings,
potentates, and those active in the affairs of cities, for these
people commit the most grievous and impious errors because
they're in a position to do so. Homer, too, is a witness on these
matters, for he has depicted those undergoing eternal punish-
e ment in Hades as kings and potentates: Tantalus, Sisyphus and
Tityus.[50] As for Thersites and any other private citizen who
was wicked, no one has depicted him as surrounded by the
most grievous punishments, as though he were incurable; he
wasn't in that position, I suppose, and for that reason he's also
happier than those who were. The fact is, Callicles, that those
526a persons who become extremely wicked do come from the
ranks of the powerful, although there's certainly nothing to

[50] Tantalus suffered everlasting punishment for stealing the food of the gods. He is depicted as standing in water within reach of the fruit overhead of a nearby fruit tree. Both the water and the fruit recede as he tries to quench his thirst and still his hunger. Sisyphus was condemned to the eternal torment of having to roll a huge stone uphill, from whence it would invariably roll down again. Tityus is represented as spread out over nine acres, with two vultures tearing at his liver. Thersites was the low-born and ugly commoner who railed against Agamemnon in council (*Iliad* 2. 212) until he was beaten down by Odysseus.

stop good men from turning up even among them, and those
who do turn up deserve to be enthusiastically admired. For it's
a difficult thing, Callicles, and one that merits much praise, to
live your whole life justly when you've found yourself having
ample freedom to do what's unjust. Few are those who prove to
be like that. But since there *have* proved to be such people,
both here and elsewhere, I suppose that there'll be others, too,
men admirable and good in that excellence of justly carrying
out whatever is entrusted to them. One of these, Aristides the b
son of Lysimachus, has proved to be very illustrious indeed,
even among the rest of the Greeks. But the majority of our
potentates, my good man, prove to be bad.

So as I was saying, when Rhadamanthus the judge gets
hold of someone like that, he doesn't know a thing about him,
neither who he is nor who his people are, except that he's
somebody wicked. And once he's noticed that, he brands the
man as either curable or incurable, as he sees fit, and dismisses
the man to Tartarus, and once the man has arrived there, he
undergoes the appropriate sufferings. Once in a while he in- c
spects another soul, one who has lived a pious life, one devoted to truth, the soul of a private citizen or someone else,
especially—and I at any rate say this, Callicles—that of a philosopher who has minded his own affairs and hasn't been med-
dlesome in the course of his life. He admires the man and
sends him off to the Isles of the Blessed. And Aiacus, too, does
the very same things. Each of them with staff in hand renders
judgments. And Minos is seated to oversee them. He alone
holds the golden sceptre, the way Homer's Odysseus claims to d
have seen him,

> holding his golden sceptre, decreeing right among the dead.[51]

For my part, Callicles, I'm convinced by these accounts, and I think about how I'll reveal to the judge a soul that's as healthy as it can be. So I disregard the things held in honor by the majority of people, and by practicing truth I really try, to

[51]*Odyssey* 11. 569.

the best of my ability, to be and to live as a very good man, and
e when I die, to die like that. And I call on all other people as
well, as far as I can—and you especially I call on in response to
your call—to this way of life, this contest, that I hold to be
worth all the other contests in this life. And I take you to task,
because you won't be able to come to protect yourself when
you appear at the trial and judgment I was talking about just
now. When you come before that judge, the son of Aegina, and
527a he takes hold of you and brings you to trial, your mouth will
hang open and you'll get dizzy there just as much as I will
here, and maybe somebody'll give you a demeaning knock on
the jaw and throw all sorts of dirt at you.

Maybe you think this account is told as an old wives' tale,
and you feel contempt for it. And it certainly wouldn't be a
surprising thing to feel contempt for it if we could look for and
somehow find one better and truer than it. As it is, you see that
there are three of you, the wisest of the Greeks of today—you,
b Polus, and Gorgias—and you're not able to prove that there's
any other life one should live than the one which will clearly
turn out to be advantageous in that world, too. But among so
many arguments this one alone survives refutation and remains steady: that doing what's unjust is more to be guarded
against than suffering it, and that it's not *seeming* to be good
but *being* good that a man should take care of more than anything, both in his public and his private life; and that if a
person proves to be bad in some respect, he's to be disciplined,
and that the second best thing after being just is to become just
c by paying one's due, by being disciplined; and that every form
of flattery, both the form concerned with oneself and that concerned with others, whether they're few or many, is to be avoid-
ed, and that oratory and every other activity is always to be
used in support of what's just.

So, listen to me and follow me to where I am, and when
you've come here you'll be happy both during life and at its
end, as the account indicates. Let someone despise you as a
fool and throw dirt on you, if he likes. And, yes, by Zeus,
d confidently let him deal you that demeaning blow. Nothing
terrible will happen to you if you really are an admirable and

good man, one who practices excellence. And then, after we've
practiced it together, then at last, if we think we should, we'll
turn to politics, or then we'll deliberate about whatever subject
we please, when we're better at deliberating than we are now.
For it's a shameful thing for us, being in the condition we
appear to be in at present—when we never think the same
about the same subjects, the most important ones at that—to
sound off as though we're somebodies. That's how far behind in
education we've fallen. So let's use the account that has now e
been disclosed to us as our guide, one that indicates to us that
this way of life is the best, to practice justice and the rest of
excellence both in life and in death. Let us follow it, then, and
call on others to do so, too, and let's not follow the one that you
believe in and call on me to follow. For that one is worthless,
Callicles.